Hooligan from the Hills
Growing Up Ornery in Iowa's Loess Hills

Jeffrey D. Deitering

© 2008 by Jeffrey D. Deitering

ISBN: 978-0-557-00040-1

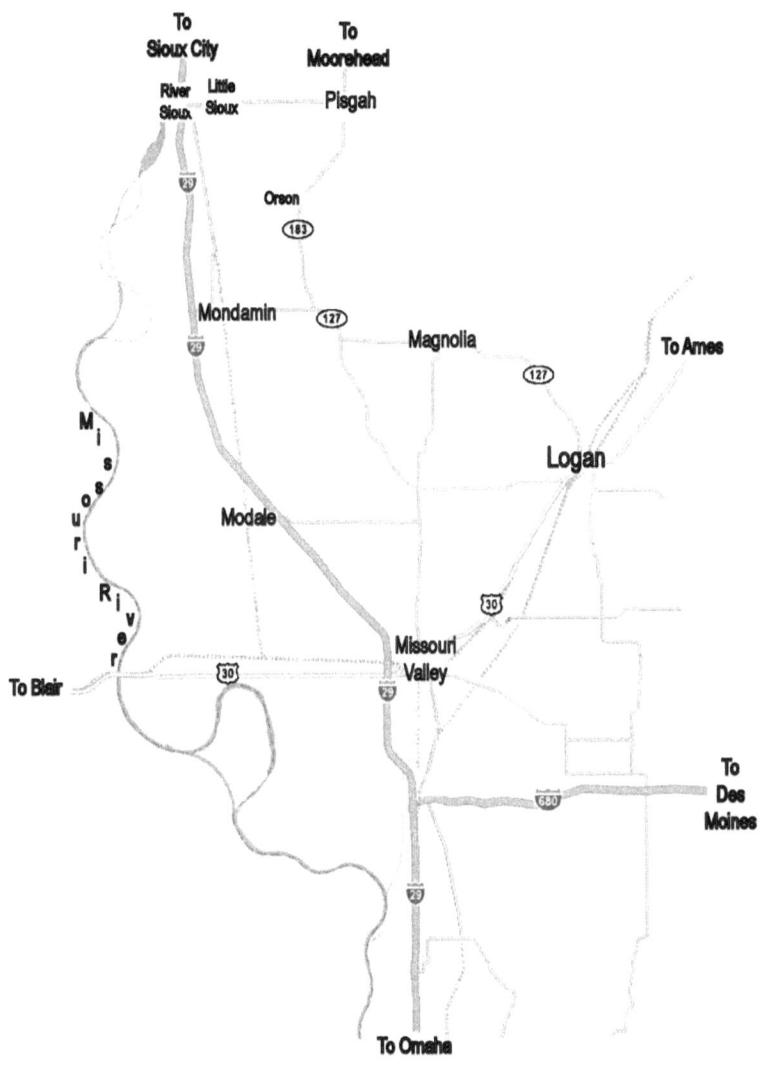

Back Home in the Loess Hills of Western Iowa

Foreword

I put together this collection of stories for the family and friends who were a part of the first twenty or so years of my life, especially the years I enjoyed in the West Harrison Community School District starting with Kindergarten in the Fall of 1973 right up to graduation in the Spring of 1986. In 1984 when Dad was awarded with a trophy at the Experimental Aircraft Association Fly-In Convention held at Wittman Regional Airport, Oshkosh, Wisconsin, the presenter announced to the audience that Dad was from "Mundane, Iowa." I felt this (presumably) unintentional slight was undeserved; the stories that follow should support my point. I've been intentionally vague with some of the names, places, and dates, but let's face it, it's a small community, and we were essentially one big family and know who did what to whom. But, I recognize there's a remote chance that some outsider may stumble across these ramblings and there's no sense in divulging all the hometown secrets now, is there?

For those who aren't familiar with the County of Harrison in Iowa, here's a quick primer on the part to which I will often refer as "Back Home." When I return from my adopted home in Kansas it's via Interstate Highway 29. The area around Council Bluffs is where everything starts feeling like old times. Twenty or so miles north of Council Bluffs just east of the intersection of I-29 and U.S. Highway 30 is Missouri Valley, a big town with a population of almost 3000 and three traffic signals (two more now than when I was cruising the loop in 1986).

Continuing another seven miles north on I-29 brings one to my first hometown of Modale. This town of nearly 300 covers the better part of 10 blocks, including the three blocks used by the grain elevator operation. Every 100 years or so the town enjoys a visit by the Missouri River which in Iowa parallels Interstate 29 and runs only a few miles to the west of Modale. When I was young Modale had two gas stations, two grocery stores, two cafes, a bank, a library, a bar, a post office, several churches, the American Legion Hall, and an elementary school for the children of Modale and Mondamin. I always drive through Modale when I go Back Home though now there is just a cafe, a bank, a library, a bar, a post office, a few churches, the American Legion Hall, the (expanded) grain elevator, and the elementary school which is now an antique shop; the rest have folded.

Both the two lane Iowa Highway 75 and I-29 North from Modale will take you to what will always be home for me, Mondamin (there is also a rail line that runs parallel to I-29 to the east that will take you to all points north but those stories are for another time). The 439 inhabitants cover most of 19 blocks though, again, the grain elevator takes up three blocks of its own. Mondamin, too, once had several businesses including two gas stations, two grocery stores, three cafes, a bank, a library, two bars, a post office, a hardware store, a welding shop, an antiquities dealer, several churches, the American Legion Hall, and the high school for the children of Modale, River Sioux, Little Sioux, Pisgah, and Mondamin. And, much like Modale, less than half remains: a gas station, a cafe, a bank, a library, a bar, a post office, a welding shop, an antiquities dealer, several churches, the American Legion Hall, the elevator, and the community school.

Another seven miles north on I-29 (or Austin Avenue) brings you to the four blocks of River Sioux and its dozens of residents. And, the great watering hole known as Ab's Place (at least it was great before the fire). The ice cream shop I used to frequent near Ab's is gone, too. East of River Sioux just one mile on Iowa Highway 301 is Little Sioux, the yang to River Sioux's yin. Roughly the same number of people as Modale, Little Sioux bettered River Sioux by having a post office, a gas station, and the gymnasium left from the days when Little Sioux had its own school.

Taking Easton Trail east out of Little Sioux will allow you to take a brief tour of Iowa's geologic wonder, the Loess Hills formation and eventually (five miles) brings you to the 20 plus blocks the over 300 people of Pisgah call home. Like the other towns, Pisgah had its share of gas stations, stores, and restaurants, half of which are now gone. Similar to Modale, Pisgah had an elementary school for the children of Sioux (both River and Little) and Pisgah. However, unlike the other towns, Pisgah had an automobile dealership (Ford), the baseball diamond used by the community high school, and, most importantly, the Old Home Fill 'er Up and Keep On Truckin' Cafe of Old Home Bread television commercial fame.

Drive south on U.S. Highway 183 out of Pisgah skirting along the base of the Loess Hills then west on U.S. Highway 127 for three more miles back into the Missouri River basin and you are back in Mondamin and have done the West Harrison lap, visiting all the communities that (then) made up the West Harrison Community School District, home of the only decent Hawkeyes in the State of Iowa. That's the setting. The character called the Beast was the rusty 1974 Chevy Blazer with full time four-wheel drive and 454 cubic inch engine that I drove with reckless abandon. And, admittedly, many of the things described here are quite stupid, however a few go above and beyond the call of absurdity and are flat out stoo-pid. I believe now the same thing that I thought that day Dad stepped up to that stage to receive his award: "Hey, it may be a lot of things but my hometown is not Mundane."

Enjoy – I did.

Be safe,
Jeff

"The world forgetting, by the world forgot. Eternal sunshine of the spotless mind!"
Eloisa to Abelard by Alexander Pope

I don't get back home much these days except for funerals but I always make sure to drive through Modale and look at the school/antique store and also stop in Mondamin at the Slab and look over at the closed Billy's Bar and Grill.

I remember sitting in the lunchroom in high school early one morning before classes and I started talking to some underclassmen about driving from Mondamin to Pisgah in about five minutes and how to cut the corners, when to drift into the opposite lane, where to watch out for oncoming traffic, etc. They were just freshmen and couldn't drive yet so even stories about parallel parking or three point turns would impress them. I distinctly recall that a freshman named Matt was one of the kids sitting at that table with me, hanging on my every word as though I was Richard Petty himself, and said something like "cool." He was killed a couple of years later in a pickup truck that was going too fast and missed a turn in the road.

I used to play what is still my favorite arcade game, Donkey Kong, quite a bit at Billy's Bar and Grill in Mondamin, often between the end of class and the start of some evening sporting event, music concert, or dramatic presentation. The owner's youngest son, a bartender and member of the West Harrison Class of 1983, did, too; he almost always held the high score. When he monopolized the machine I would watch intently, trying to divine the secrets of his game play that allowed him to be so much better than the rest of us. I have the game on my home computer and whenever I play it I still say to myself "this is where Rick jumped twice to get that extra 100 points." Don't ask me why I remember this sh-, er, stuff, I just do.

Seems like a lot of the stuff I remember from school was stupid or dangerous - usually both - and I struggled with which stories would be appropriate to retell without encouraging anyone else to try the same dumbass things. When I had the privilege to speak to the West Harrison High School Honor Society a few years ago my main theme was "lead by example because you never know who is watching you and just what it is they are seeing." I finally decided I don't have all that much influence over time and space or my fellow human beings so what follows are tales of both good and bad.

I learned a lot of extremely arcane and useless things during my thirteen years in the West Harrison Community Schools. Here are a few that can't be found in any textbook:

1. An Interstate "Rest Area Next Exit" sign is bigger than a 4'x8' sheet of plywood. Much, much bigger.
2. Taco Bells are (were) made of fiberglass and do not ring.
3. The best breakfast to be had is (was) a donut from Keith's Store and a can of Pepsi.
4. Nothing will ever compare to a tasty Ash Burger made by Netty at the Office Bar and Grill in Mondamin.
5. Al's gas station at Little Sioux doesn't I.D. for alcohol purchases if you are tall enough to look over the counter
6. The Blair Movie Theater didn't I.D. much, either.
7. A dumbass in a pick-up truck power-braking with studded snow tires on a Mondamin sidewalk will leave a pretty deep gouge in the concrete.
8. Fireworks are more fun on Halloween than on the 4th of July.
9. Tinfoil has many uses.
10. Pink flamingo yard ornaments are not as prevalent in Harrison County as one thinks.

"All in all it's just another brick in the wall"
Another Brick in the Wall, Part 2 – Pink Floyd

In Miss Allen's Kindergarten Class in 1973 there was one toy for Play Time that was by far the greatest toy ever produced. They were just a little bigger than shoeboxes, though similar in proportion, and were decorated with a multicolored brick pattern. They were toy building blocks. Really big ones. They were the Big Blocks.

My best friend, Mac, and I used to play with them every chance we got. Miss Allen had made flash cards with color pictures of each toy available for playtime. One had to be the first to choose the card to play with that toy, sort of like checking out a rental movie today. I was the class dolt and was the last holdout in the learn-to-tie-own-shoes category and Miss Allen always encouraged me to take the card for the toy boot (a wooden model boot with real laces on it) to practice my shoe-tying skills. I would have none of that during Play Time. "Any time you want to practice, you just take the boot and keep trying" was the encouragement she once gave me. I tried to take her up on that one day during Music Time 'cause I wasn't very keen on singing; that's the day I learned that "anytime" doesn't always mean *anytime*. Miss Allen's "anytime" didn't include Music Time and my "anytime" didn't include Play Time: impasse. We had to agree to disagree. Mac and I often hid the Big Block card so no one else would get the card - and the big blocks - first.

There was an issue, however. Mac and I used to build really tall walls and pillars that towered over everyone in the classroom (except, of course, the adult Miss Allen). We had to stand on one of our desk chairs when Miss Allen wasn't looking to complete the "topping out" of the structures which were at least three and a half – maybe even four - feet tall. Problem was, after creating such engineering marvels the only thing left to do was, naturally, knock them down. Demolition, after all, is a natural progression from Construction. Monster sized Legos in concept, except they lacked the round prongs to really hold things together, meaning great care was required during construction but made demolition really, really, easy. You wouldn't think that a bunch of cardboard boxes would make such a racket, but they did. After just a few weeks of playtime creation and noisy destruction, Mac and I were banned from playing with the Big Blocks. The much-deserved Big Block banishment lasted just a few weeks for us; we regained our building permit only after we agreed that there would be no more disruptive dismantlings.

I saw Miss Allen a few years ago and had the opportunity to tell her that I became a Civil Engineer in part because of that quality Play

3

Time spent constructing and deconstructing those large capital projects built using the Big Blocks.

In 1997 I again thought of the Big Blocks and those "tall" walls and monoliths that Mac and I built over thirty years ago as I was walking across a steel beam 235 feet above the ground in my duties as a field engineer on the construction of the Airport Traffic Control Tower at the Kansas City International Airport. It is one of the tallest buildings in the Kansas City area. I was scared witless but at least my steel-toed boots' laces were tied properly (yes, Miss Allen did finally learn me up good on the shoe-tying thing). For a few moments I was able to calm myself enough to enjoy the view of the airport below me and catch a glimpse of the Kansas City skyline some fifteen miles to the south. I smiled. I couldn't help but think that in thirty years or so when the building has outlived its usefulness that I would have to give Mac a call and have him come to K.C. to help me knock it down - if Miss Allen would let us just this one last time.

**"Darling, come take a seat
You can always eat at Joe's"**
Eat at Joe's – Suzy Bogguss

One recent Saturday morning, one of the McWilliams boys mentioned a few memories of being raised around Modale, some of which had nearly completely faded from my memory. Like getting a pop at Fat's. Fat's garage/gas station, the large, galvanized sheet metal building there at the terminus of County Road F50 and Main Street at the center of town, with its huge main garage door in front seemingly always open. Dad said that the pop machine in Fat's place would dispense a soda for a nickel. And, when the distributor raised the price so that a pop would cost a dime, instead of paying to upgrade the coin mechanism on the machine to take a dime, Fat put a cup on top of the machine. The listed price of a pop went up to 10 cents: when you put your nickel in the machine you were supposed to drop a nickel in the cup, too. But, that's not what I remember about Fat. Whenever Dad and I went into the garage Fat would always give me a stick of Juicy Fruit gum from an open pack that he usually had in the top drawer of his desk. There were a few times he didn't have any gum - he said that some kids had broken in and stolen it and I always believed it. In retrospect, he was probably just out of gum, but that's not nearly as interesting a story.

Also mentioned that morning was Joe's Store. At one time there were two stores in Modale: Harlan's and Alexander's. When Harlan retired that left just Joe and Gertie Alexander as the town's sole purveyor of sundries. As a small child I always thought the two story gray metal-clad building with small round windows that housed Joe's store was actually a Missouri river boat that had grounded itself next to the Modale American Legion Hall. He had a little bit of everything in that store and my Gramma D. thought he sometimes altered expiration dates to on the food packaging to a more recent year - though that was never proven. I was with my buddy, T.C., one day when he bought a single pack of Topps baseball cards that had a Reggie Jackson card in it - the only time I ever saw anyone get a top-name player from a store-bought package of trading cards. Dad and I usually grabbed a bottle of pop from the pop cooler and a well aged Hershey bar off the shelf. And, sometimes a model car (as I said, Joe carried a little bit of everything) that we would put together a little bit at a time each night for weeks.

Now Joe's Store is closed and after Fat passed away, the fuel pumps were pulled out from the front of the garage. I asked Mom and Dad what Fat's name really was. They didn't think they had ever heard him called anything else. Grandma M. didn't know either. Dad called my Aunt Bev and she couldn't remember. She said to call Snick

Kinart. For those who haven't seen Snick on Good Morning America, Mr. Kinart is a Modale resident and area icon. One who has lived in the area for over 100 years? Not only has Snick seen a century worth of local history, he remembers it all in vivid detail. So, Dad gave him a call. Not only did Clarence George "Fat" Middleton come right off the top of his head (apparently Clarence was a portly child and picked up the nickname when he was very young), but also Snick had some other interesting observations. For instance, the dry spell we had in the Midwest during the first part of 2006 apparently is virtually the same weather pattern that Snick remembers occurring in 1934, 35, and 36 - the Dustbowl years. The farmers back home took advantage of the unusually warm weather and were able to disk the fields starting in late January. Mr. Kinart says that never in his lifetime has he seen farmers working the land in January and February like they did in 2006. When a centigenarian says something like that, I start to be concerned. I know that a hundred year sample period out of 4.5 billion years of weather isn't really a statistically significant indicator of weather change, but you still have to wonder about this alleged global warming the theorists have been going on about...

Snick, by the way, was born Earl William, and people started calling him "Snick" when he was just four weeks old. (Earl W. "Snick" Kinart, age 105, of Modale, Iowa, passed away on Friday, September 28, 2007).

"Hey, Joe, Where You Going with that Gun in Your Hand?"
Hey, Joe – Jimi Hendrix

Each and every day Miss Allen's Modale Kindergarten class was concluded with all of us sitting on the floor around a large writing tablet on an easel. We would pepper Miss Allen with things we recalled happening during that particular day and she would write them down - sort of a large scale diary. Or, to put it in more contemporary terms, an analog blog. (Thirty years later and I still do this except now it's in meetings and not always done on a flip chart and easel; sometimes we use a white-board and call it "brainstorming").

After drafting the day's diary entry, Miss Allen placed a similarly sized chart on the easel that had every student's name on it. She would go through all the names and decide whether or not each student had been "good" that day. Someone who had behaved well got a star for the day, those who had misbehaved got no star. Every five stars earned a person a small piece of candy. It wasn't a big piece of candy but we weren't big people so it was an incentive to walk the straight and narrow. I thought it was great at the time (it was pretty rare for someone to not get a star for the day). I'm sure this could never be done today: someone would surely complain about the type of candy given (peanut allergies, anyone?), about the damage done to misbehavors' psyche when they didn't get a star, about giving candy to everyone so no one feels left out, or maybe not giving out stars or candy to anyone and prescribing Ritalin or some other depressant to the obviously ADD children (despite Miss Allen's sugar laden reinforcement, I believe we all turned out just fine).

There is one diary entry in particular which stands out in my memory both because of the event's uniqueness and because Miss Allen uncharacteristically embellished upon the actual event. It was the last day of classes before Christmas Break (yes, it was still "Christmas Break" then and not the more secular "Winter Break" of today). That day we had our little party and did our gift exchange. It's been over thirty years so I don't remember the particulars of who had whose names. I do, however, remember that someone had given Mac a dart gun as a gift. So far there are so many parts to this story that could never happen today that it almost makes me cry. A Christmas Party at a PUBLIC SCHOOL?! GIFT EXCHANGE!? A toy WEAPON at school with the TEACHER'S KNOWLEDGE?! My goodness, how did our class ever graduate?

Anyhoo, I digress. Despite the rampant political incorrectness of the day, we were all playing with our toys when the principal, Mr. Bolte,

7

decided to make an unannounced visit to our classroom, presumably to wish us all "Merry Christmas and Happy New Year." (Festivus for the Rest of Us had not been invented yet) Sadly, we will never know for certain what his intentions were. Mac was only five years old and had not been through Hunter Safety training yet. Who can really blame him for not yet knowing that after he loaded that dart in his gun that he should have kept the muzzle pointed to the floor and his finger off the trigger? It was a bit of impeccable comic timing that would have impressed even the great Mack Sennett. The gun muzzle was casually waved about the room. The trigger was accidentally pulled. The dart flew straight and true, and Mr. Bolte was struck on the left hip. Of course, the suction-cup tipped dart bounced harmlessly off the bottom seam of his gray suit coat, but the startled look on his face was priceless. The room became deathly quiet; we were certain that Mac was about to receive the Principal's wrath, whatever that may be. However, without saying a word, he turned in the doorway and left straight away. I don't know that he ever spoke a word of the incident.

That event was the closer for the class diary that cold, December afternoon. Miss Allen, teaching us at a very early age how to evoke drama by using just a little artistic license described the event as: "Mr. Bolte came to our room and was shot in the heart by a dart." Such violence and drama at the tender age of five. Who'd a thunk Mac would move on from this "tragedy" and end up in the Peace Corps helping thousands of underprivileged people half a world away?

Remember: Treat ALL guns as if they are loaded, keep the muzzle down and away from people, the finger off the trigger, and be safe.

**"The fundamental things apply
As time goes by"**
As Time Goes By – Herman Hupfeld

RIF – Reading is Fundamental. I distinctly recall seeing the Public Service Announcements during my Saturday morning television shows (Beep..Beep..Zip..Tang!!) touting this book give-away program that was created in 1966 by a retired schoolteacher. I asked my mother why there wasn't a RIF in our area. She told me to go to the library. Point taken.

In the Modale Campus' Kindergarten classroom was a "large" (large to a 5-year-old) ferris wheel made of pine and plywood, painted in flat navy blue and bright red with yellow accents. It was a couple feet wide, stood nearly five feet tall, and had bookshelves where the ferris wheel seats would normally be. This was what passed for the Library for our first year of school. That wooden behemoth probably could have easily removed one of our limbs if any had ever gotten pinched in it but, oddly, that likely event never occurred. The greatest book available in that wooden ferris wheel that held the story books in Kindergarten was "Giants Come in Different Sizes." It was so popular that the cover was broken and the pages were literally falling out of the book. It was about an island that had been cursed and was covered by a dark cloud. The people who lived there contracted some giants to come to the island to remove the cloud for them. It was the last giant who was the largest - and had a cold - who sneezed and blew the cloud away. For reasons I don't comprehend, I never forgot that book and finally was able to purchase my own copy of this out-of-print book just after my 38th birthday.

Our first reading textbook was *A Duck is a Duck*. I still have a copy of it; yellow cover with a picture of a duck in the center of it (There are copies available through used book stores for around $3 plus shipping). In one of our Second Grade readers was an excerpt of a book I later read in whole called *Flat Stanley*, the story of a boy flattened in a tragic falling bulletin board accident who survived but was only wafer thin. About that same time I read another book called *The Mouse and the Motorcycle* about Ralph the Mouse who rode a toy motorcycle. Mrs. Carrier, our third grade teacher, read to us every *Boxcar Children* book available in 1977 but it's the first book in which they actually lived in the boxcar that to this day remains my favorite. Our fifth grade teacher, Mr. Van Pelt, read us several stories but the two I remember most are *Andrew the Big Deal* (I have a signed copy of this one) about a klutzy kid from a family of athletes who moves to a new place and finally grows up, and *Black and Blue Magic*, a story about Harry Houdini Marco who gets a magic lotion that allows him to grow wings and fly - I've also got a copy of this book now. In the fourth grade one of our classmates lent me a very worn copy of *James and the Giant Peach* that was much better than the movie that came out a few years ago. The Area 13 book exchange and the Mondamin Public Library (also known as the "Pub_ic Library" whenever someone stole the "L" from its sign on the front of the building) gave me access to a whole hoard of 1940's and 50's era science fiction that often grossly overestimated what technology would be like in the 1980's. When we were both in junior high, my friend, Morrow, from the Pisgah campus introduced me to the *Dune* trilogy. Another friend, Big Al, talked me into reading Tom Clancy's *Red Storm Rising* which led me to reading the entire Jack Ryan series to its implausible conclusion. Now, I've come somewhat full circle and am reading kids books again and am hooked on the Harry Potter series.

Even though one of our junior high instructors, Mrs. Johnson, once chewed me out for rushing through assigned math problems so I could get back to a book I was reading, I still believe reading has served me better than some of the lessons we were given. Although RIF is now most often used for "Reduction In Force" (a euphemism for "layoffs") reading is indeed still quite fundamental.

"When through the woods, and forest glades I wander, And hear the birds sing sweetly in the trees."
How Great Thou Art - Carl Gustav Boberg

I think we were in Kindergarten when went on our first school field trip. Of course it wasn't earlier but it may have been First Grade - I'm getting old and my memory is getting a little fuzzy on things that we did thirty-four years ago - but I'm thinking it was Kindergarten. For the sake of this voyage in the way-back machine, it was the spring of 1974.

Kids in Kindergarten at the West Harrison Elementary/Junior High School campus at Modale went to the Henry Doorley Zoo at Omaha for their field trip. Beats the tar out of me what our future classmates at the Pisgah campus did for a field trip, my attention was only focused on my little slice of the planet.

Because we were a group of twenty-one five year-olds we couldn't be trusted to explore such a big space with only Miss Allen and a couple of volunteer parents providing chaperon power. So, the Fourth Grade class also came along too. I imagine someone thought this would be a good idea for a couple reasons. Economy of scale: one trip, one bus, two classes. Added supervision: the buddy system would be employed and each Kindergartner would be paired with a Fourth Grader for the day. Like the Bowl Championship Series and Socialism, this was better in theory than in practice.

Random drawing, alphabetically, tea leaves, I don't remember how the hell we were partnered up, just that for that one day I was supposed to be "buddies" with a Fourth Grader named Jay Durnil. The joy and excited anticipation of going to the zoo for my first time was instantly replaced by dread. Although he was four years older than I, I was already very aware of my "buddy." "Bully" was the first word that came to mind. I was certain that the entire day would be filled with taunts, insults, and slugs to the arm.

A bit of luck fell my way just prior to the day we visited the zoo. Jay broke his leg (tibia fracture, I think) and ended up with a cast on the lower half of his right leg. By the time we actually boarded the bus to head down I-29 to Omaha to go to the zoo, he had healed enough that he could put weight on the leg and hobble sufficiently to get around. Mobile, but not too quick. My spirits lifted; there was a good chance I could out maneuver him and escape the brunt of his wrath.

It turned out I worried for nothing (a habit I've been told I still have today). Jay was just as excited to visit the zoo as I was, so much so that he totally forgot his ornery ways and acted more like a friend than a foe, often pointing to the animals to make sure I saw everything he was seeing.

I have two distinct memories from that day. One was the disappointment we all had when we entered the building that was the home of Casey the Gorilla. This was 1974 and the notion of providing zoo animals large areas similar to their natural habitat to roam was just coming into vogue but the renovation of the gorilla and orangutan buildings was still a decade away and 30 years before the Hubbard Gorilla Valley would be constructed. What we saw that day was a thick pane of glass that separated us from Casey. Glass that Casey had, in a fit of gorilla rage (probably from hearing that renovations were delayed), had scratched so badly that we couldn't see anything other than claw marks. No gorilla for us that day.

My second memory from that day was watching Jay Durnil, the bully with a broken leg, smiling and laughing, and often leading the two classes down the concrete paths, hobbling as fast as his plaster covered leg would allow, to be the first kid to see the animals in the next exhibit. I'm not going to say that I left that day with a new best bud - this was the real world and not an after school special - but I did see Jay a little differently. That day we had fun.

He moved away after that school year ended, to the town of Elkhorn just outside of Omaha. It was about a year later that he was abducted and murdered, found on the bank of the Missouri River, a case that is still unsolved. My young mind didn't understand it then and my old brain doesn't understand it now.

I know there have been a lot of additions to the zoo since I was in Kindergarten: an aquarium, an aviary, a veldt for the big cats, and an expanded area for the gorillas. People look at me strangely when I tell them I haven't been to the zoo in decades even though I lived just thirty-eight miles from it. I probably will visit it again some day; it is the one of the best zoos in the world, after all. I'm just not ready yet.

"I'm Snowblind, Snowblind, Snowblind"
Snowblind - Styx

Occasionally, we get a little bit of bad weather here in my adopted home state of Kansas. As they are wont to do, the weather folks on the television love to predict doom and destruction of near epic proportions. They are usually only marginally wrong. Once, we did, in fact, get some freezing rain. However, depending on which part of the viewing area one lives, the paralyzing snowstorms that sometimes get predicted either drop a foot of the white stuff or, such as usually the case at my house, just a fluffy dusting that doesn't even cover the sidewalks.

Nothing compares to the disaster that we experienced Back Home in January of 1975. For most of my life I associated that blizzard with Kindergarten but we were actually in first grade when it hit. Either way, it was a big unscheduled break from going to school. We lived out in the country northwest of Modale at that time. The official snowfall was somewhere between 12 and 24 inches but the 60+ mile per hour swirling winds created snow drifts that were as tall as our house. Now I know that the wind-chill at the time was around 80 below zero (Fahrenheit, no metric crap here).

That didn't stop me from going out into the storm, though. The drifts in the backyard by the windbreak that dad had planted were five feet high or taller - well over my six year-old head -- and several had nearly vertical faces just begging for a kid to go tunneling. This is what I did. Bundle up, scurry from the front door to the closest drift, punch a gloved fist through the outer crust of the drift (like breaking a Styrofoam cooler), then create a snow cave to escape the brutal wind that was more frigid than a woman I briefly dated my junior year of college. Although it was probably just a few minutes, I remember just laying there in the snow cave I created staring into the whiteout outside, listening to the wind howl for what seemed like hours. We ended up getting much of the second week of January off from school because of the abnormal amount of snow and the unusually high drifts that were created. I spent much of the time turning our backyard drifts into Stalag 13, tunneling everywhere possible until the sun turned it all into one big, sloppy puddle.

That storm is still my benchmark for bad weather. I haven't seen bad weather for 30 years. However...

...reset the Wayback Machine to a bitter cold winter day in 1977. Three classmates and I had made plans to ditch school that day. Shoot, the kids on the TV did that all the time so why couldn't we. Of course, those fictional characters lived in big fictional cities with lots of interesting fictional places to visit. Not exactly the same case in the Village of Modale, but, hey, we were only 8 or 9 and what the heck did we know.

Anyways, detailed plans were made for what was sure to be the greatest escape since, well, the *Great Escape*. Except with no motorcycle and the whole freakin' world was the cooler. It was a far from simple escape plan. The first stage wasn't going to be too bad: ride the bus to school just like usual. Next, when the other kids walked west across the gravel parking lot to the school we were to instead break to the north and circle behind the wooden shed used as the bus barn. Once behind the barn and out of sight, wait until the coast was clear then run a few more yards to the north just beyond the school yard fence to the edge of the creek. Then we would have to carefully follow the creek to the south, staying low below the creek bank so as not to be seen by anyone looking out the hopefully frost covered windows. The final leg of the escape was to skirt the fence that separated the Engins' yard next door from the schoolyard and head back east away from the playground to freedom. Then it would be a simple jaunt across country to Troy's house only a couple miles away. The perfect plan; what could be simpler?

When the day arrived, Mac and I decided that the freezing temperature and the sub-zero wind-chill were not optimal for executing the plan just to blow off a day of school. If there had been even a hint of snow that day school would have been canceled, but since it was just bitter, arctic-cold, it was business as usual. Logic dictated the plan should be delayed to a more hospitable day. Inexplicably, Paul and Troy decided to bolt anyway. Mac and I knew it was a bad idea but we were certain they would come to their senses and come back to school. They didn't.

The weather that was needed to cancel school began not long after class began. We really started to get concerned when the wind began to blow even stronger with occasional bursts of snow and sleet. We hoped that if they were going to continue to be too stubborn to give up and come back that maybe the weather would at least break but it just continued being bitterly cold and windy.

It was a couple of hours later when Mac and I finally got worried enough about them out in the even further deteriorating weather that we went to our teacher, Mrs. Strain, to tell her what we thought they had done. It took a little convincing to get her to believe that some of her kids would do something that damned stoopid. Once she believed us she went straight to the principal so they could wring their hands together while trying to figure out what to do. Two children supposedly trekking across frozen farm fields in near blizzard conditions; no solutions immediately came to mind.

Mac and I were convinced they would freeze to death while the adults tried to decide what to do. Not to worry though, a hunter from Modale out snowmobiling found them crossing a cornfield near Troy's house. Despite the dismal conditions the plan had nearly worked and they were almost within sight of their final objective. But, they were freezing cold, had minor frostbite, and were quite happy to be found and given a ride to the rest of the way to Troy's house. They were also in deep doo-doo. But, they did get the day off. And, the next one, too.

"We Have the Technology"
Opening Dialog of *The Six Million Dollar Man*

One of my classmates, Juan, appeared in a photograph in the January 6, 2006, U.S. News and World Report. Those of you who were on Annual Staff with me know that the magazine's not identifying the people shown in the picture would earn the deep ire and a stern admonishment of our yearbook editor. I believe our friend from the West Harrison Class of 1986 is the soldier on the left riding in the rear of a Stryker armored vehicle patrolling the streets of Mosul, Iraq, although it is extremely difficult to determine because of the combat helmet, sunglasses, and full body armor the two Airborne Rangers shown in the photo are wearing.

Juan is one of the youngest members of our class; his birthday being sometime near the beginning of the school year. One day at the start of our first grade year, Big Juan was running around the Modale playground during the morning recess telling anyone - and everyone - who would listen that he was not just any man but *the* Six Million Dollar Man. Being 1974, that particular Lee Majors television show was very popular (it had not yet jumped the shark with its Bigfoot episodes). I thought that running around claiming to be "bigger, stronger, faster" seemed a bit boastful, so I had to ask what was up with the six million dollar man stuff. He said, "I'm the Six Million Dollar Man and you're the Seven Million Dollar Man." I was only a first grader so the subtle nuances of his statement sailed right over my young head; I was still baffled. He then explained so even my little noggin would grasp it. "It's my birthday. Today I'm six. You're seven. Get it?" Finally, I "Got it." By that logic, I guess now we're six times better, stronger, faster, than we were then, but most of the time I sure don't feel it.

When we were in third grade, Big Juan got his hand pinched in a door (or some other classroom danger) which would have brought tears to most any other kid, but Juan just shrugged it off. Our teacher, Mrs. Carrier, asked him if he was all right to which he nodded his head. Then she asked him again to make sure because she said she knew he was "a tough man who never complained when he was hurt." Not a bad reputation to already have earned at the age of eight.

Before shipping out to his last assignment in the Middle East, Juan told me he was the tip of the sword. My hope is the training Juan received both as an elite Commando in high school and as an Airborne Ranger in the today's Army keeps him safe while dodging sniper fire and improvised explosive devices in the most dangerous combat zones of the world.

17

"Turn Out the Lights the Party's Over"
The Party's Over – Willie Nelson

In 1976 Miss Levine was our Second Grade teacher. She only taught for a couple of years at West Harrison, having taken over for Miss Woodard who had transferred up north to the Pisgah campus. I thought Miss Levine was pretty cool and was very disappointed when she got engaged – couldn't she have just waited another 15 years or so for me to hit the market?

Anyhoo, while Miss Levine (now Mrs. Walker) was on her honeymoon we had a substitute, Mrs. B. Twenty-three seven year-olds can be a handful, and we were every bit as rambunctious as we could possibly be the whole time Mrs. Walker was gone. I believe during Mrs. Walker's honeymoon I saw for the first and only time a substitute break down in tears because the class was so unresponsive.

The party ended quickly, however, when Mrs. Walker returned. Not only was Mrs. B's report on our behavior disparaging enough, but also Mrs. Carrier, next door in the Third Grade room, filed a complaint about how loud and disruptive we had been.

Another first for me at that time: I believe Mrs. Walker was just a hair's breadth of literally exploding when she saw us that first morning after her honeymoon. She was so embarrassed by our disrespectful actions that we were sentenced to copying passages out of our reading books. We did this all day long for three days, only breaking for lunch. Recesses were officially canceled for two weeks; about 10 times the normal punishment for bad behavior.

After the first three days of copying words, she reduced our sentence to just doing words during what would have been our recess time. Boy, howdy, did that ever suck.

I remember when the 2:30 bell rang ending recess time on the Friday of that second week of punishment and several of us broke into smiles (a couple of people even clapped quietly). She blew a gasket again "All right you 'yay'ers,' keep doing words until the end of the day." To this day I have never been called a "yay'er" again and wonder why anyone this side of sanity would willfully become an elementary teacher or, worse yet, a substitute teacher, and put up with the likes of us.

"Gentlemen, you can't fight in here! This is the War Room."
President Merkin Murffley in the movie *Dr. Strangelove*

My interest in aviation began at an early age. My Grandpa Maule used to tell enthralling stories about his tour of duty with the Army Air Force and flying as a waist gunner on a B-24 Liberator in the European Theater. John Wayne taught me that the coolest Army Air Corps fighter airplane ever built was the P-40 Warhawk which he flew in the movie *The Flying Tigers*. But, what really fueled my early infatuation with aviation, warbirds in particular, was the annual open house at Offutt Air Force Base in Bellevue, Nebraska. Dad took the family every summer to see the static display aircraft and also the afternoon air show. The SR-71 Blackbird, the British Avro Vulcan, the AV-8 Harrier, the A-10 Warthog, the B-52 Stratofortress, depending on whether it was an Air Force or a Navy year, either the Thunderbirds in their T-38 Talons or the Blue Angels in their A4F Skyhawks, and the flagship of SAC: the continuously airborne EC-135 Looking Glass. Bellevue was the home of the Strategic Air Command and once each year we saw a great deal of the Strategic aircraft.

What I remember most vividly, however, was not the magnificent wonders of flight but the protesters who always stood outside the base gates protesting the event by picketing. As we drove away one year in the late 1970's, there was a person outfitted in a Death costume with a hand-lettered sign attached to his Scythe that read "Did You Enjoy Your Weapons of Mass Destruction?" As others honked their horns in derision, I remembered hearing Dad say, "Yeah, I think we did." It was a pretty cool show, in the sky, on the tar-mac, and outside the gates.

That was also, though, the first time it occurred to me that living only fifty miles from the most important Air Force Base in the Midwest wasn't necessarily the safest place to be. The Cold War was at its pinnacle so the daily threat of nuclear attack was a feeling we already knew all too well. True, "Duck and Cover" hadn't been taught at the West Harrison schools for a number of years but everyone within 100 miles of SAC knew that after Washington, D.C., Bellevue/Omaha would be on the short list of places to be destroyed next. Furthermore, who in their right mind believed all the Inter Continental Ballistic Missiles those technologically crude Rooskies designed and built would actually land directly on Bellevue? I mean, hell, our nukes were built by the lowest bidder and their stuff was inferior copies of our cheap work so it was obvious that even though we lived 45 miles away, there were bound to be a few strays and we were most assuredly toast.

We saw the missiles that would be used against us every spring when the news broadcasts showed Moscow's May Day Parade. Even the television miniseries *The Day After* (filmed in part in my adopted home of Lawrence, Kansas) showed us what horrible deaths awaited us from radioactive fallout. The movie *Red Dawn* confirmed that Omaha would be wiped out. *The Phantom from 10,000 Leagues* and *Mothra* gave us a glimpse of what terrible beasts would arise from the inevitable nuclear event. I decided at an early age that if we ever got a warning that an attack had been detected I would drive to Omaha to make sure I was incinerated immediately instead of just made painfully ill and dying slowly and miserably. Every time the television went to a snowy static I wondered if that was a problem at the station's transmitter site or if the pre-attack electromagnetic airburst had been detonated. Such is the overactive imagination of a child in the 70's. It wasn't until President Reagan triumphantly dismantled the U.S.S.R. that I stopped thinking of such things. Now I just wonder if the FedEx truck parked in front of my office building will explode as I walk by it or if a letter in my In-Basket will contain a biological agent. If we have to have enemies, I think I prefer the Russian Army instead of a bunch of cowardly religious zealots - at least the Commies respect MAD (Mutually Assured Destruction).

Remember: In case of nuclear attack, Duck and Cover.

"We'll send him cheesy movies
The worst we can find"
From the opening song of the television show *Mystery Science Theater 3000*

One of the highlights of the Saturday nights during my youth was *Creature Feature*. Back when my folks used to go east of Missouri Valley to the Desoto Bend lake with the Cleavers, the Snyders, the Smiths, and many others, to boat and water-ski, we would get home and have the lake gear stowed just in time to flip on KMTV Channel 3 broadcasting from Omaha and catch *Creature Feature*. Back then KMTV was an NBC affiliate but *Creature Feature* was a locally produced show. It came on at 10:30 right after the local news. Hosted by the wild, red haired, green make-upped, and bloody lab coat wearing Dr. San Guinary and his off screen monster sidekick, Igor, *Creature Feature* was the *Mystery Science Theater 3000* of 1970's Omaha television [NOTE: Dr. San Guinary was in the 1974 Modale Centennial Parade]. Dr. San Guinary showed only the best: *Tarantula*, *Abbot and Costello Meet Frankenstein*, *Dracula*, *The Invisible Man*, and other greats from the 1940's and 50's. Every ten to fifteen minutes there was the obligatory commercial break but that was OK because before the movie resumed, there would be a short skit by Dr. San Guinary and Igor. Watching during the summers was fairly easy but once I started Kindergarten staying up to watch became much more of a struggle. I was worn out from those long days of being educated at West Harrison's Modale campus. That and my folks had the misguided notion I needed to sleep more during the school year. So, although I liked the show, I didn't get to watch it every week. In fact, in 1975 not long after I started 1st Grade, I didn't manage to stay up on a single Saturday night to watch.

It wasn't until Valentines Day weekend in 1976 that I was able to force myself to suffer through the talking heads doing the local late news to watch the good doctor and his faithful henchman. But, it was worth it, 'cause once the news guys (no women allowed on the news at the time) signed off I knew some old B horror or sci-fi flick hosted by the doc would air. But, instead, some live video of a theater stage and band was shown. Didn't look too scary to me. Then some chubby guy was riddled with machine gun fire and rolled down a stairway onto the stage. It was announced that this was "Live from New York" and that it was "Saturday Night." Well, no duurrr. I knew it was Saturday night and I wanted my crummy old spooky movie and schticky Dr. San Guinary (and Igor). What a stinky load of festering crap.

I found out later that the Doc had been moved to midnight after this other stoopid show rolled its final credits. No normal seven year-old could stay up that late and I couldn't either. I was as pissed-off as a

23

little kid could be. At least the AWA professional wrestling was still shown on Sunday mornings; no problem being awake for that. It would be another three or four years before I started to appreciate the juvenile "brilliance" of *Saturday Night Live*, a show I still watch today (well, record and watch the next day 'cause I still can't stay up late enough to watch it "Live").

Creature Feature finally went off the air in 1981, but Dr. San Guinary continued to make personal appearances at charity and public events for many years after that. John Jones, the wonderful man behind the make-up, passed away in 1988. Whenever I watch an old B ghost story, I still hear "Ah Ahhh" of the Doc and Igor's moaning roar in response.

**"At the good ole rock and roll road show
I gotta go"**
Saturday Night – Bay City Rollers

In the early 70's I was up before dawn every Saturday morning - it drove my mom nuts. For some reason, *Scooby Doo* followed by the *Bugs Bunny/Road Runner Show* were always on at the crack of dawn – before the crack of dawn during the winter months. What the heck was up with that? Those sadistic bastards at the networks started me down the path of Chronic Fatigue Syndrome at an early age 'cause those were two of my favorite shows.

Fortunately, for the days I overslept I had some backup shows that were almost as good.

There was *Devlin*, the motorcycle stunt riding carny family who traveled around the country performing death defying feats and also solving mysteries. *Devlin* was on in 1974 when the popularity of Evel Knievel was at its pinnacle.

There were several live-action shows I watched with regularity (almost all produced by Krofft or Filmation) such as *Shazam!*, the ongoing travels of Billy Batson a.k.a. Captain Marvel and his aged driving buddy, Mentor, RV-ing about the country fighting crime (nowadays that old perv, Mentor, would probably be a member of NMBLA) Isis, which was basically *Shazam!* on estrogen with a much more attractive lead.

In college my dorm floor watched Deidre Hall play Marlena on *Days of Our Lives* but when I was six years old I watched Deidre Hall on *Electra Woman and Dyna Girl*, a female version of Batman and Robin.

How about the übercool twelve-wheeled SUV traveling the post-apocalyptic earth on the show *Ark II*?

The first colossal pop and roll sellouts of my memory (*Monkees* don't count) were the Bay City Rollers who (briefly) had their own variety show on Saturday mornings – my good friend and classmate, Lisa, was inexplicably a huge fan.

A group of miniaturized kids were constantly searching for a way to return to normal size while evading the evil scientist on *Dr. Shrinker*.

Before Dan Akroyd and Bill Murray crossed the streams and roasted the Sta-Puft Marshmallow Man, there was Larry Storch and Forrest Tucker "Zapping" spirits and monsters on *Ghost Busters*.

For those of us too young or too obedient to Nancy Reagan to try hallucinogens there was the psychedelic world of *H.R.Pufnstuf*.

Years before he was Gofer or an Iowa Congressman, Fred Grandy was fighting crime with the help of Dracula, the Wolfman, and Frankenstein's Monster on *Monster Squad*.

I still carry a torch for Cadet Gentry, a member of the small class of students on that wayward asteroid known as *Space Academy*.

Speedbuggy was an animated suped-up dune buggy but in the live action world we had the *Wonderbug* (same show, different medium).

And, my favorite of the "live" shows on Saturday was the precursor to *Jurassic Park*: the *Land of the Lost*. A few years ago there was a person who worked in my office who, no kiddin' now, was named S.Lee Stack. Every time I saw her nameplate I thought of those hissing bi-peds in the *Land of the Lost*. Oh, Marshall, Will, and Holly, won't you ever get home????

"God, Jackie! We can do that for the rest of our lives! Star Wars is a limited engagement!"
Michael Kelso on the television series *That 70's Show*

Thanks to the Westroads movie theaters in Omaha and to the new (then) twin screen theater in Blair, there were some pretty good films we got to see when we were in high school. However, for every *Vision Quest* there was a *Hot Dog...The Movie*. For each *For Your Eyes Only* there was a *Top Secret*. Every *Silverado* was countered with a *Rustlers' Rhapsody*. The *Sudden Impact*'s were coupled with the *Night Patrol*s. The insulting Black Moon Rising accompanied the brilliant Repo Man. 1955 looked really cool in *Back to the Future* but *The Adventures of Buckaroo Banzai Across the 8th Dimension* was seven dimensions too many. Eddie Murphy was at the height of his game with *Beverly Hills Cop* but Chuck Norris was on his way to pushing exercise equipment after *Lone Wolf McQuade*. We saw so many bad movies in the 80's I can't even remember if *Big Trouble in Little China* was the good and *They Call Me Bruce?* was the bad or vice versa. At least *Red Dawn* foreshadowed our fate if World War III broke out: Omaha got nuked.

In 1977 a goofy looking movie called *Star Wars* came out. There wasn't much of an advertising campaign but the wingnuts on both coasts had gone gaga over it. The news programs on all three of Omaha's TV channels we had available to us showed several fluff news clips of weirdoes standing in huge lines - many wearing strange costumes - to watch this film over and over and over again.

Mom and Dad took my sister and I to Omaha to see this movie at the Indian Hills theater that (at the time) had the largest screen in the region. And, it had a type of stereo sound that was supposed to be superior to the quadraphonic stereo sound of the 8-track player in Grandpa's Lincoln Continental. Regardless of the quality of the story, the movie going experience was always top notch at the Indian Hills.

Even though we were just no-nonsense Mid-West folk the line was still pretty long. Thinking back on it now it really wasn't much of a line, certainly not anything like the ones in the east and west metropolises (metropoli?) that had been shown on the national news shows, but having never stood in line for just a movie made it long to me by default. We had heard about the silliness of the rabid fans this movie had instilled, but we actually knew nothing about the movie itself other than it was science fiction.

I assumed it to be better than the average movie or people wouldn't want to do the previously unheard of: pay to see it more than once.

Needless to say, with such unprecedented hype, my jaw nearly stuck to the sticky, soda-soaked cinema floor when the film began – began by showing TEXT! What kind of movie starts with words – lots and lots of words? Holy Library Card, Batman, if I wanted to read I would have checked out a stinkin' book. I was starting to have severe reservations when the shot slowly panned down the star filled screen to give us our first view of the desert planet, Tatooine. Then the first two star ships filled the whole freaking screen. These weren't just the cheesy models from that old television show called *Star Trek*, these babies made you *believe*. Believe that spaceships weren't just cone-shaped capsules that needed oceans to land, believe that robots didn't all look like Robby and get all flustered when that dipstick, Will, was in danger, believe that if we just lived a long time ago in a galaxy far, far away that we, too, could be a part of an interplanetary struggle against the evil Empire.

Well, what 9 year-old's life wasn't changed then? And, the toys. Those little dolls – *action figures* – every kid had at least a couple of them even though they were too small and were minimally articulated. What, no elbows? No wrists? They couldn't even hold the tiny accessories and weapons that came with them. But, I still have the little Darth Vader with its orange light saber concealed in his unbending right arm I got nearly 30 years ago. Because I took him out of his packaging, though, he is worthless to anyone else but me.

I've been a movie addict ever since. And, when Lucas began "tweaking" and re-releasing his original three *Star Wars* films in 1997, you're darned right I took the day off from work, stood at the very front of a huge (no, really, it was) line, and was in the audience for the very first showing of the new and "improved" *Star Wars* in Kansas City. Unfortunately, this time around the movie was slightly different. Some scenes were added (good), some scenes were altered (not good – everyone over the age of 30 knew Han Solo fired first), and the whole film was redone to be clearer (very good). The improved clarity was paramount because this time I was watching the movie on a modern screen. "Modern," of course meaning a dinky, little screen. I really miss the stately Indian Hills theater. I understand there's a strip mall in its stead. Too bad. Big movies deserve big screens but big chains rarely build 'em that way anymore.

As a kid in the sticks, television viewing consumed a possibly unhealthy significant portion of my free time. Sure, I also read hundreds of books, but, sadly (but not regrettably), I watched a lot of the TV.

Fads go in cycles (I like to state the obvious) which is a shame because belted tee shirts and leggings are trying to come back into style. As a toddler, the Western genre ruled the boob-tube. *Gunsmoke* lasted 20 flippin' years, well past Miss Kitty being even remotely attractive. Seems like that map of the Ponderosa was burned every week for about as long.

When I entered grade school police dramas such as *The Streets of San Francisco*, *The Rookies*, *Adam 12*, and the like (with the tangential private eye shows like *Barnaby Jones*, *The Rockford Files*, and *Cannon* thrown in as filler) filled prime time and reruns. It's hard to write some of those names without adding "A Quinn Martin Production" at the end.

Junior High school was the time of science fiction. Although *Star Wars*, my favorite movie, just had its 30th Anniversary, I declined to celebrate because its creator has become the king of merchandising and a sultan of reissues, having not told a compelling story since the Empire struck back. However, riding the *Star Wars* coattails onto the small screen were *V*, *Space 1999* (actually predating *Star Wars*), and *Battlestar Galactica*.

Sitcoms seemed to take over for a while ("Must See TV on NBC" got my attention every Thursday night). I'm hoping the aberration that is staged "reality" television dies an excruciatingly painful death - soon - and that a 100th incarnation of *CSI* called *CSI: Ankeny* never materializes. Somehow we have skipped Westerns and have cycled back to the age of police dramas.

I thought of this triviality as I stumbled across a rerun of the original *Battlestar Galactica*, thankfully at the end of the episode. I had forgotten that, although groundbreaking in the special effects arena (for a television show), the potentially interesting plot line was rendered impotent by sappy stories told each episode. Good thing Maren Jensen and Laurette Spang were in the cast or the show would have been unbearable to watch. The irony of the old show reappearing in syndication is that the new and improved version just announced it is ending its run this season. Bummer. I'm still waiting for an explanation of how the Cylons' eye got built into the hood of K.I.T.T.

And, yes, I do know what the original *Star Trek* intro is "to boldly go where no man has gone before" but all the reading I've done and several excellent english instructors taught me long ago that this is a grammatically incorrect sentence. To quote Mrs. Perly, "before you can break the rules you need to first know the rules." Captain Kirk used a split infinitive every week and to this day it still bugs me a little bit.

"Fleeing from the Cylon tyranny, the last Battlestar, *Galactica*, leads a ragtag, fugitive fleet, on a lonely quest—for a shining planet known as Earth."

My only hope is that if and when they find Earth, they aren't so disappointed they return to the Cylons and surrender.

**"Oh, no! We can't stop here! This is a
two-dimensional planet and the
children can't manage here!"**
A Wrinkle in Time by Madeleine L'Engle

It's my recollection that it was Paul who pushed the prank just a bit too far. Mrs. Strain's stepped out of her 4th Grade classroom for a couple of minutes one morning and someone jumped onto the counter under the bookshelves, reached up, and moved the minute hand on the classroom clock ahead a couple of minutes. The class giggled nervously. That made us a smidgen early for morning recess, which caused Mrs. S. to wrinkle her brow. And, we entered the lunchroom shortly after the 3rd Graders, which caused a bit of a traffic jam at the food counter.

The first person back to the classroom after the noon recess jumped onto the counter and reset the clock even further ahead. We arrived at the gymnasium for Physical Education just as the previous class went down to the locker rooms to shower and change back into street clothes - we were almost ten minutes early which confused the Phys Ed instructor, Mr. White, a bit.

When we got back to the classroom Mrs. S. wasn't in the room so Paul jumped up and pushed the clock even further ahead. I think we all - including Paul - knew this was not going to end well, but when you are only ten years old you really live for the moment. Mrs. S. appeared a bit befuddled when she returned to the classroom - she had gone to look for us because we were "late" in coming back from P.E.

Technically our school day ended at 3:30 but because most of us rode a school bus the day ended earlier. Kindergartners left their classroom to get onto the school buses around 3:12, First Grade left around 3:15, Second Grade headed out at about 3:18, Third Grade left their room at 3:20, - you see the pattern. When done correctly the buses loaded smoothly and kids didn't get grouped up and rowdy. I think it was when we, the Fourth Grade, went outside and queued for the buses behind the Kindergarten Class that Mrs. S. had an epiphany.

She used to try to teach us a lot of that hippy-ish New Age crap that she was learning in some Masters course she was taking, stuff like "Warm Fuzzies" and "Cold Pricklies" which were just cutesy euphemisms for praise and derision and how these made people feel. Well, duh. As we boarded the buses about 15 minutes early that day I swear I heard her drop a few cold pricklies on us. Yeah, there was heck to pay the next day but it sure was funny that day.

I can't say for certain that this episode influenced my maturation process but to this day I have every timepiece over which I have control set 10 to 12 minutes fast; I much prefer being too early to missing the bus.

"School's Out for the Summer"
School's Out for the Summer – Alice Cooper

The last day of classes for the seniors at the West Harrison Community Schools is usually in mid-May; the rest of school always goes on another two weeks. I don't know if it was the same for those who went to grade school at the Pisgah Elementary School, but the last day of class on Modale Elementary campus meant two things: 1) everybody rode their bike to school (about a seven mile ride for the kids who lived in Mondamin), and, 2) squirt gun fights after school. The bike ride was only a couple of miles for me so the only trick left was not getting my squirt guns confiscated.

Water weapon technology in the late '70s was not nearly as sophisticated as it is now; there were no Super Soakers or any other high capacity/high pressure/high volume dowsers. We only had the extremely fragile, leaky, brightly colored pistol replicas that held about a thimble full of water and had the range of about three feet. So, it wasn't too big of a deal when one of these $.75 wonders was taken away by a teacher. Except, then you were totally defenseless in the H_2O battles.

One year I managed to not lose my pistol (a lime green Luger shaped model) by taking to school a stack of old comic books bound together with string - the squirt gun was concealed in a hole in the center of the stack I had made by cutting out portions in the middle books similar to what I had seen in numerous wild west films. I shudder now to think of what extremely rare and (now) highly collectible comic books I ruined in the name of water warfare.

Another year I gutted a water pistol for its inner plumbing and glued the parts into one of the small plastic rectangular pencil boxes most of us used to keep our, well, duh, pencils and stuff. Even with a whole tube of model glue I couldn't get it watertight. Since I had procrastinated until the night before the last day of school and this effort failed miserably, I had to resort to just a regular water pistol which was confiscated by our sixth grade teacher and notorious curmudgeon, Mrs. Johnson. Damn.

A few daring souls would snipe a few shots during the school day but the real battle didn't begin until school let out. Once outside the building, pistols would be drawn, and it was on. But, the meager capacity of those crude water guns only lasted a few shots and then needed reloading. The only supply available was the water hydrant in Modale's city park located across the street to the east of the school grounds. He who controlled the hydrant controlled the water war. Not only was the hydrant needed for refilling the pistols but also for filling water balloons: saturation bombardment was critical for defense of the hydrant as well as for retaking the hydrant position when it was lost. Most importantly, a strategically placed thumb under the spigot would turn the hydrant into a water cannon of unlimited supply. It took a well-coordinated group assault of water pistol and balloon tossing to capture the hydrant. Alliances would be formed and dissolved as needed to wrest control of the hydrant away from whoever had it.

As eager as we were for that end of the school year to arrive, we would stay at the same school grounds for an extra hour, drenching each other before finally leaving for home soaked from the perfect end-of-year celebration and start of summer kickoff party.

"It was like lightning, everybody was frightening"
Ballroom Blitz – The Sweet

Seems to me the Missouri Valley Roller Rink reopened around 1977 or so, when I was in the 4th grade. It was on South 5th Street just north of the railroad tracks. I'm pretty sure Larry was the name of the guy who ran the place. At first the floor was its original gray paint and was a bit rough, but not long after reopening it was stripped and sanded down to the original tongue and groove hardwood surface. A smooth surface was imperative for the roller skates of the time: leather boots with two pairs of hard urethane wheels, a pair in front and a pair in back. These seemed a lot less forgiving to pebbles than the softer wheels on today's all-terrain in-line skates.

If you didn't own skates there was a vast array of rental models available: black skates for guys, white skates for ladies, and little kids got dingy tan skates. Most of the rental skates were set up to be pretty stiff. The "plate" (the metal chassis on the bottom of the boot) had adjustment nuts that could be reset to allow the front pair of wheels and the back pair of wheels to pivot more freely, making it easier to do sharp turns. That adjustment also made it easier to fall down. But, if you were a frequent customer of the rink and were on Larry's good side he would loosen the skates up a bit if you asked.

During 4th and 5th grade I spent most of my fall and winter weekends skating there, sometimes waiting at the door for them to open in the morning and being one of the last to leave the hardwood at the end of the evening. Who'd a thunk rolling counter clockwise for five or six hours at a time would be so entertaining? NASCAR, I guess.

The rink seemed huge at the time but I've been inside the building since it changed hands and now realize that it wasn't much bigger than a basketball court. The entrance opened into a cattle chute that funneled us to the cash register and skate rental desk. After paying and getting skates you would turn right to the lobby/changing area which had benches for changing out of shoes and into the skates and also had places to hang jackets, coats, and the like. The bathrooms were in this area, too. Left of the register was the snack area. It was at the roller rink where I learned what a fountain pop suicide was: Pepsi, Orange Nehi, Dr. Pepper, and 7-Up all in one cup - Larry would mix it but don't dare take it outside the very small snack area. God help the kid who spilled a pop or dropped a piece of candy onto the rink's hardwood.

Separating the snack area and changing space from the rink was a low wall that formed a semicircle with just a narrow opening in the

35

arc's center to allow access to the skating area. The longest outside wall was cinderblock painted blue on its bottom half and white on its top. Its opposite was, too, but also had a full-length wooden bench for rest stops without leaving the skating floor. The far wall was square to the long walls where turning traffic would leave natural open areas in the corners that were usually used by novices trying to learn how to stay upright. Although there were no lines painted on the floor anymore, it was just understood that the middle of the oval was for skaters to spin.

Music was played non-stop, all vinyl 45s spun on a turntable, the sound blaring through a few in-ceiling speakers. Mostly disco crap and current pop'n'roll shtuff. Is there anyone over the age of thirty who didn't learn how to do the "YMCA" semaphore at a skating rink? There was also the Rick Dees classic "Disco Duck" to which we would crouch down onto one skate and stick the other skate straight out in front while keeping it off the floor (called "shoot-the-duck") - a skating style that would was also useful during the limbo.

From the white lay-in ceiling hung a disco ball in the center of the rink and equally spaced around the perimeter were the numbers 1, 2, 3, 4, 5, and 6. The numbers were for something called the Dice Game that was a variation on Musical Chairs. Everyone would skate around the rink while music played and when the music stopped the skaters stopped under one of the numbers. Then Larry would throw a monstrous stuffed die. The group under whichever number came up from his toss got to stay and everyone else left the floor. Then the music restarted, the skaters resumed skating around the rink and when the music stopped, again the die was tossed, more people left the floor, etc., etc. until only one person was left who won either a pop or a free pass to skate. Great fun and a little foreshadowing of the gambling that would be a part of Iowa's future.

The disco ball was used for two purposes: the couples' skate and the Snowball, both of which were extremely traumatic. For the couples' skate you had to man up and ask a girl to skate with you while the lights were out and music like Bette Midler's "The Rose" played sappily over the sound system. If you weren't flat out told to go to hell you might skate hand-in-hand, or, if you found a partner who skated really well, the boy would put his hands on the girl's waist and the girl would put her hands on the boy's shoulders, the girl skating backwards the whole time - or until their feet got tangled up and they both crashed to the floor. The Snowball was as bad or worse because it started with one couple skating and the separating at the sound of Larry's whistle to go find two other partners from the dregs sitting on the bench along the wall. Much like being picked last for kickball, it sucked sitting on that bench hoping to be chosen.

I feel as though I know Chubby Checker's "Limbo Rock" by heart because it played over and over and over while we skated under a limbo stick at least once and sometimes twice a skate session. "Older" kids only had a chance if they first skated a circle around the limbo pole and then shot-the-duck, leaning into the center of the circle they had just skated, counting on momentum and centrifugal force to keep them from tumbling while flattening out to go under the stick. Usually the contest was won by a girl less than five years old who was able to do the splits and shuffle her skates enough to slide under a limbo stick less than a foot above the floor.

The speed skate time was always a blast. Normally, if you skated too fast and/or recklessly, Larry would blow his whistle and tell you to slow down or, worse yet, sit down for a while. But, twice a session for the length of The Sweet's song *Ballroom Blitz* he would allow groups of skaters, usually grouped by age and ability, to skate as fast as they possibly could. I think this is how the floor got cleaned, too, because a kid wiping out at full tilt would tumble quite a ways and pick up a whole lot of dust. At least I always did. I took a few lessons on speed skating/racing which is where Larry taught us to run on our toe stops for the first ten feet to start and that the best way to stop is to turn around quickly and, while rolling backwards, hop up onto the toe stops. Believe me when I tell you that neither of these is to be tried on in-line skates.

I was such a little skate freak that when the rink had its skate marathons (12 hours of roller skating with only a smattering of 5 minute breaks) I was there at the front of the line waiting to get into the rink. Two stinky little feet riddled with blisters were well worth a small plastic trophy and a coupon for one free skating session. I have three of those trophies.

I don't know if it was the increasing time demands of being a teenager or if it was the rink going out of business that caused me to stop roller-skating. It couldn't be that I outgrew it. Anyhoo, now the Missouri Valley Roller Rink is the Missouri Valley Eagles Club and it is available for parties, wedding receptions, family reunions, and the like. No skates required - or encouraged.

Doe Sigh Doe
Oh, Johnny – Billy Mooney

A rainy day 25 years ago meant our Physical Education class would be held in the gymnasium. P.E. in the gym usually meant either whiffle-ball or dodge ball on scooters. But, there was also the much more sinister P.E. section held indoors that lasted for what seemed like months: dance. Is it any wonder that so many of the guys in our class became wallflowers after three solid weeks of Square Dancing for Dummies?

The intent was to teach us rhythm but, good night, couldn't we have been taught some form of dance we may actually use somewhere in our lives? Though disco had recently perished, I believe the final exam was to do the Hustle. The stress of having to pair up with a girl – ones who had only quite recently cured their cases of cooties – was agonizing. These were girls we had known since before Kindergarten and were more like family than dance partners – what if they got the impression that we may actually like them?

And, if that wasn't bad enough, the music was immeasurably worse. Sweet Sony Walkman, the music we endured would have flushed Noriega out of his office in a matter of minutes. Worse than any one-hit-wonder, the music to which we were taught to "dance" was etched into my gray matter with an ice pick. The mental anguish of having to perform antiquated dance "moves" to those relic LP's played on a portable, single speaker turntable scarred me for life. I was able to write out the last five lines of the square dance classic *Oh Johnny* call from memory today. Let me repeat: nearly 30 years later and I was able to write out the last five lines of the *Oh Johnny* square dance call from memory TODAY. That's just wrong. And, worse yet, never once did it increase my ability to get a date. Ever. Not in the least. EV-VER.

As excruciatingly painful of an experience as it was for me at the Modale school, I can only imagine the plight of the Pisgah students being taught rhythm and all the hippest square dance and polka moves by their oh-so-svelte Phys. Ed. instructor. I'm sure seeing his three bills of girth "gliding" across the gym's hardwood to some lame polka tune recorded on a wax cylinder back in the late 1800s would damage a person in ways from which one could never hope to recover.

You all join hands and you circle the ring. (Circle right)
You stop where you are and you give her a swing. (Swing partner)
And now you swing that girl behind you.
Go back home and swing your own right where you find her.
Allemande left with the girl on your left.
Dos-a-dos your own.
And now you all promenade.
With that sweet corner maid.
Singing Oh Johnny! Oh Johnny! Oh!

Oh Johnny- Billy Mooney

"Blinded Me with Science"
Blinded Me with Science – Thomas Dolby

There were many drawbacks to having elementary schools on separate Modale and Pisgah campuses: sports teams too small to compete, redundancies in staffing, band and chorus groups with too few members, etc. I thought the biggest drawback, though, was that for the first nine years of school, we never got to know the classmates with whom we would eventually graduate. Except for people like one of the two Angies and Becky who attended both schools, we rarely interacted.

However, because of 4-H, parents, and how the buses ran near my home, I got to meet some of the "other half" of our class before we all became freshmen at the unified high school. Like in 7th grade I went to the Pisgah Science Fair. My friend, Morrow, a future engineer, was going to be showing off his new Tesla Coil, which I actually wanted to see. And I also knew the Angies (both of them), Missy, and Becky would be there and it was always good to see them. Always.

The fair was in the Pisgah gymnasium. When I got there the basketball court was covered with tables and tables of typical junior high science projects. And, at mid court on a rubber floor mat, were Morrow and his coil.

A Tesla Coil is an electric device that discharges high voltage, high frequency energy, much like lightning. This was pioneered by the inventor Nikola Tesla who envisioned one day building coils that would be capable of transmitting power and information all over the world without using wires. His dream was crushed by energy brokers who recognized that giving power to consumers without wires would be impossible to bill. Some people were convinced this man-made lightning would be too dangerous to use.

This is what I remember about that Science Fair. While Morrow was lighting up fluorescent light tubes by placing them near the coil and making his hair stand on end by waving his hand near the electromagnetic field, he was also receiving occasional shocks. You could always tell when this happened because Morrow would swear - understandable, Mr. Nurse, the rotund Physical Education and Science instructor would tell him to watch his mouth - as expected, and Bobby and his pal Puggy would laugh their butts off - naturally.

Bobby and Puggy weren't just passive spectators they were active participants. While the budding engineer was having fun with high voltage, they would come up behind him and, while standing off the rubber mat, would stick a metal rod up near his ear causing an arc of electricity to jump from his ear to the rod.

Arc, shock, profanity, admonishment, and giggles. Repeat. Definitely the must-see demonstration at the Science Fair. I don't know how much was really learned by all this but Morrow - despite all the shocks - still became an electronics engineer. And, I got a photograph of Becky and me, arms around each other's waists (yep, PDA) that I still have. A good time had by all.

"I Tip My Hat to the Keeper of the Stars"
Keeper of the Stars – Tracy Byrd

Dena (Globe) Keckler (7/11/68-11/24/00), you have not been and never will be forgotten.

I was preparing to send an email and saw an entry in my address book I will never have an opportunity to use again. All the people in my life are special in their own way though you never really think about it until the opportunity has passed. This is for my friend Dena.

Dena was my first "steady" girlfriend in the fifth grade. She was a pretty, blue eyed, blonde and one half of a set of identical twins. Girlfriends up to this point were just childish relationships - the girl you slugged in the shoulder the most or maybe ignored more pointedly than the other girls. But, fifth graders got to attend fifth and sixth grade dances that were occasionally thrown at the old American Legion Hall. It wasn't mandatory to have a significant other to attend but not many attended stag so you really needed to bring your own dance partner. So, after the requisite note passing and "check this box if you'll be my girlfriend" being checked in the affirmative, Dena was my first girlfriend, and accordingly, my date to my first boy-girl dance.

We met at the Hall, of course; that's just how fifth grade dates were: you were taken there by your parents, you left with your parents, and your "date" was the time in between. It was a Christmas dance, that first one, where there were chips and punch and crappy post-disco techno pop music. And, there was a sprig of mistletoe strung up in a secluded corner of the dance floor. Dena gave me my first real kiss at that dance under that mistletoe. Like most pre-junior high romances, our courtship only lasted a few weeks, a few kisses. I can't say I remember them all but I do remember the excitement and anticipation of trying to steal a few moments for her kiss.

Much as our "relationship" began, it ended with a check-box marked "no." Twelve year olds' hearts are resilient: our next significant other was only a note-pass and check-box away; I'm relatively certain that Dena helped me draft my next "check-here-to-be-mine" tome.

We finished elementary school, junior high school, and finally high school together, never "dating" again after fifth grade, but always remaining friends. Like so many other of my high school friends, I fell out of touch with Dena when I left for college. We got together once when I was back home from Iowa State and she let me tag along with her and some of her nursing school friends to a country dance bar. I didn't know how to two-step so I just stayed at our table and guarded the ladies purses while they were on the dance floor. It was the first time I wished I knew how to two-step.

After that night I never really talked to her much until our tenth high school reunion. We exchanged email addresses then and ever since I have sent her all manner of jokes, puzzles, and other electronic junk that everyone gets. And, in kind, she sent me pictures of her new daughter, inspirational stories, and soulful poems.

I feel so empty now, seeing how I squandered the chance to tell her anything of substance. I've always thought by forwarding humor to others that I might be putting a smile of their face. Now, I don't feel I've really accomplished that much at all. A good friend of mine taught me how to two step and I think to myself whenever I'm out on the hardwood "See, Dena, I can dance now."

"Mount St. Edelite. Leonard Bernstein. Leonid Brezhnev, Lenny Bruce, and Lester Bangs"
It's the End of the World as We Know It - REM

I was creating an internet-based form the other day and had to make a list of state names for an address field. Naturally, it was quite easy to type up all fifty - in alphabetical order, no less. Not because of any geography class but because of Mrs. Shelton's music class.

"Fifty, nifty, United States, from thirteen original colonies. Scout 'em, shout 'em, tell all about 'em. One by one, 'til we've given a day to every state in the U.S.A." To this day I have to run through the song from Alabama to Wyoming to remember the states.

Another song that still haunts me is that awful ditty about some dumb-ass named Henry and his piece-of-crap bucket: "Henry: There's a hole in my bucket dear Liza, dear Liza. There's a hole in my bucket dear Liza, a hole. Liza: Well, fix it dear Henry, dear Henry, dear Henry, Well, fix it dear Henry, dear Henry, fix it." About fifteen verses of detailed instructions on pail fixing later we are again reminded that Henry the Incompetent Boob has a hole in his damn bucket.

And, while on the subject of poor saps with their own songs, who can forget the five o'clock shadow of Mike Finnigan? "There was an old man called Michael Finnigan, He grew whiskers on his chinigin. The wind blew them off but they grew in again, Poor old Michael Finnigan – Begin again:" Seems like this song would never endigin.

My classmate from the Pisgah campus, Aileen, is a much more cruel and vindictive person than I ever could have imagined. Not satisfied with the "catchy" songs I listed above, she reminded me of the hippy-ish *Up with People* song from the traveling show of the same name. I could only remember the second verse (below) but discovered via a Google search that hundreds (thousands?) of other people have the song tattooed into their gray matter as well.

Up, up with people
You meet them wherever you go.
Up, up with people
they're the best kind of folks you know.
If more people were for people
and people everywhere
There'd be a lot less people to worry about
and a lot more people who care.

Aileen, also reminded me that we never had enough song books to go around so Mrs. Shelton always had to write out all the music and lyrics on the chalk board, even all twenty-something verses of that stoopid Michael Finnigan song. Knowing how these tunes have stuck with me - and, apparently others - after only a few years of exposure, I can only imagine what kind of long term damage Mrs. S has suffered after more than two decades of listening to tone deaf little kids singing them.

"That'll Keep You Going for the Show
Now Come On It's Time to Go"
Comfortably Numb – Pink Floyd

I have not been back home for Holiday Concert time at the West Harrison Community School in quite a number of years. However, I can still recall the concerts in which we participated a few decades ago. And, I'm pretty certain it was called a Christmas Concert back then.

At the Modale Elementary campus the concert festivities always began with an open house. The Kindergarten through Fourth Grade rooms downstairs were decorated with all the crafty crap we had done in our art classes - and almost all of it was blatantly Christmas themed (in your face ACLU). Upstairs the junior high rooms were likewise decorated though in a more skilled and subdued manner - hey, we only had art a couple of times a week in the big kids grades.

Anyways, even though the open house/concert was on a Wednesday (or Thursday since Mrs. Shelton and Mr. Scharff conducted both Modale and Pisgah schools' music departments and the concerts at both schools couldn't be on the same night) both students and parents were dressed in their Sunday best.

After milling around the classrooms viewing the handiwork of the children the parents, grandparents, aunts, uncles, cousins, friends, and the other three people left in the community wandered up to the gymnasium and took seats in the wooden stationary bleachers along sides of the basketball court or in some of those metal folding chairs (normally used to smash professional wrestlers over the head) that were placed down on the court proper.

The grade school kids would sit in one section of the bleachers closest to the stage, grouped by class. The students in each class were arranged in an order that was determined at the dry run done during that day's practice session; usually a one line human bell curve with the taller kids in the center tapering down to shorter ones out at the edges.

The fifth and sixth grade band and chorus and the Junior High band and chorus gathered in the band room and lunchroom respectively. I remember that my classmate, Lewey, said to me before our last Christmas Concert that he had put on extra antiperspirant that night and was sweating worse than if he had used none at all.

The order was always the same - as were most of the selected songs. The lights in the gym would dim, the curtains would pull back, and the Kindergartners who had left their places in the bleachers would emerge from the wings and take center stage. Looking past the basketball hoop hanging just above the stage the Kindergarten class would start things off with a stirring rendition of such yuletide classics as *Frosty the Snowman* or *Jingle Bells*.

The weeks of preparation seldom showed though the perennial First Grade favorite of *All I Want for Chrithmuth ith My Two Front Teef* did require a lot of practith to get the lithp down.

Two songs per class, Kindergarten through Fourth, with songs getting slightly longer with each class. Since we had split elementary schools at that time the classes rarely had more than twenty-five students, which usually meant a handful of talented voices carrying the rest of us? Remember to smile, everybody, and watch Mrs. Shelton at the piano who will be mouthing the words as she plays the accompaniment.

After what had to be an unbearable amount of caterwauling (to those not related to the participants) it was then on to the bands and choruses (chorii?). The combining of the 5th and 6th grades and the 7th and 8th grades improved the vocalizations somewhat by doubling the talent – those of us who were/are tone deaf knew enough to keep our voices down or just lip-synch altogether.

The bands were, well, the bands were about as good as you can expect a thirty-piece concert band to be. I write about this because an unnamed classmate who attended a recent holiday concert asked me "did we sound that bad?" Probably. I remember times when people were off a few beats, when someone would play through a rest, when a natural could be clearly heard when it should have been a sharp, or even when someone would miss a coda and just plain go off on a tangent from the rest of the band. Any one of those things would sound awful. But, I also remember times when all the sh - stuff came together, when we the whole band was on the same beat of the same measure on the same page playing in the same key and the sound was just so right that it gave me goose-bumps. Yeah, sometimes we sounded as bad as Lisa's band on *The Simpsons*. But, there were also times when we sounded every bit as good and professional as the Boston Pops. To me, anyway.

Oh, and hey, Lewey: Me too, and it still seems to work like that.

"He conquered fear
and he conquered hate,
He turned our night into day
He made his blazing saddle
A torch to light the way..."
Blazing Saddles – Frankie Layne

At the Modale campus, each year the day before Christmas break started, the teachers treated the students with a movie. The tables in the lunchroom would be moved aside and a portable Da-Lite movie screen would be put up in front of the serving counter. The movie projector, a battered green and black educational Bell & Howell 16mm Filmosound with a single built in audio speaker, was set up in the center of the lunchroom. The tables, metal tube framed with the white Formica tops and integral benches that folded up in the middle to be easier to roll around and store, were oriented to be makeshift bleachers, albeit extremely uncomfortable ones.

The movie was something ordered from Area 13 resource center but the teachers sprang for sodas for us when we were in Junior High, the only day the whole school year we were allowed to have pop in the building.

The school watched the film in shifts. Kindergarten through Second Grade watched during the morning while the "older kids" did classroom busywork. Third through Sixth Grades watched next. The last showing of the day was reserved for the Junior High students to watch the movie and drink the sweet forbidden nectar of caffeinated, carbonated soda.

I recall getting in trouble for holding hands with Alisa during the movie when I was in 8th grade (busted by one of our Junior High instructors, Mr. Ulrich) though I don't remember what the movie was that year. There was never an official Code of Conduct when we were at Modale in elementary school and junior high but it was pretty well known the Public Displays of Affection were frowned upon. But, hey, when you're only 13 years old about the only time you get to see your significant other is at school or a school function so you had to make the most of your time together. Besides, I still maintain it was entrapment: *they* turned off the lights; what was I supposed to do?

As for the cinematic selections, I specifically remember watching the Bob Hope classic *The Paleface* one year (not very Politically Correct by today's standards but considered pretty darned funny – by Caucasians - back in the day) and the Don Knotts masterpiece *The*

Incredible Mr. Limpet one other year. Ahhh, nothing says "Christmas" like a racially insensitive western-comedy or an animated fish.

For those interested in reliving the grade school movie going experience, you can buy a vintage Filmosound from various sources on the internet for less than $50. A decent portable Da-Lite screen suitable for projecting films in an elementary school lunchrooms will set you back at least three times that amount.

**"Mental wounds not healing
Who and what's to blame?"**
Crazy Train – Ozzy Osbourne

Many of you who went to school with me predicted it and in the summer of 2005 it finally happened. After blatantly baiting the system regularly over the last 19 years the Man finally caught up with me and I was in court. Yep, after registering and voting in darned near every local and national election in every place I've ever lived since turning 18, I finally got called upon to perform county jury duty. And, ironically, because I now have so many friends in the law enforcement field, I was deemed unworthy, didn't make it through the preliminary screening process, and was sent home early. The buffoon of a defense attorney must have assumed that I wouldn't be able to relate to the accused's perspective. As Split used to explain very graphically at the chalkboard (chipping the chalk with emphasis) "Never ASS-U-ME."

Spending the better part of the day in the Douglas County Courthouse made me think of punishment, which, quite naturally, reminded me of our 8th grade field trip to Des Moines to see the State Capitol and tour the Living History Farms.

Getting up at 4am that day wasn't so bad - shoot, I do that every day now. Since there were about 46 of us including chaperone's we took that POS (Piece of Stuff) Bluebird bus, the one with the flat front that struggled to achieve the legal speed limit of the time of 55 miles per hour, especially if there was a stiff breeze or a slight incline (our classmate, Paul, swore that some kid on a tricycle pedaled past and on ahead of us as we went across the state on Interstate 80).

The Capitol tour was OK, especially when I snapped a photograph of the governor's chandelier after being told "no pictures." The Living History Farms visit was interesting enough, particularly the old gentleman at the General Store who showed me a walking stick that was actually a rifle (have a picture of that, too). A quick look around at the Danish Windmill in Elk Horn gave us enough time to buy those goofy Viking hats with the Styrofoam horns sticking out the sides. All in all, spending the entire day with our mostly unfamiliar classmates from the Pisgah Elementary campus actually made for an entertaining excursion (reunited with my Kindergarten sweetie, Angie, at last).

It really was a fun trip, except for that damnable tape recorder that my friend T.Roy brought. That, in itself, wouldn't have been so bad except he only brought one cassette to play. Really, T.Roy, why just ONE?! *The Blizzard of Oz.* And, why did you only play the beginning of *Crazy Train*. "All aboard! Ha, ha, ha, ha!" A newish twist on music that was even then already a bit dated. "All aboard! Ha, ha, ha, ha!" The Oz-man, post Black Sabbath, but before Randy Rhodes died. "All aboard! Ha, ha, ha, ha!" Some consider it a classic. "All aboard! Ha, ha, ha, ha!" Ozzy before he was an aged caricature of his former self. "All aboard! Ha, ha, ha, ha!" Why the hell couldn't we just hear the WHOLE FREAKING SONG? "All aboard! Ha, ha, ha, ha!" I will always hate that song's intro and opening guitar lick; after all we all heard it several hundred times during that 289 mile round trip. "All aboard! Ha, ha, ha, ha!" Thank the maker the batteries finally, mercifully died, along with any affinity I had for that song. "All aboard! Ha, ha, ha, ha!"

"Who says you can't go home?
Who Says You Can't Go Home? – Bon Jovi

I went back home one Sunday for the afternoon. As usual, I drove through Modale to see how things have changed. It was good to see that a new stop sign was put up in front of Vittitoe's; I'm sure the farmers hauling corn/soy beans to the grain elevator really appreciate having one more opportunity to test their brakes and task their engines under fully loaded conditions. It shouldn't take too long for washer boards to appear in the pavement in front of the intersection.

But, I digress. I cruised past the old elementary school and found that the antique store that utilizes the building was open for business. Even if I didn't already possess a penchant for perusing the wares of every antique shop I stumble upon during my travels up and down I-29, I would have stopped anyway just to see my old school.

First off, the antique furniture in the main shop areas on the second floor seemed to be of a better condition and quality than most of the other places I've been. But, then again, the prices were quite a lot higher than most places, too. The as-is/needs repair area that takes up the entire gymnasium was absolutely amazing. There was stuff covering virtually every inch of the basketball court and every last bit of seating space in the bleacher areas on both sides of the hardwood floor.

My wife and I only looked an hour but could have spent much more time there – and probably will some other day. But, really, the antique thing was really just a subterfuge to allow me to explore and reminisce in our old school building.

Our old school has not weathered time very well since 1982. There are several places where there are obvious leaks in the roof, especially in the gym where a lot of the roof framing is now exposed (I always wondered how they built the half-cylinder curved roof and now I know). The lower half of the building is closed off to the public - I think the store owners live in that part - and me, being public, didn't get to wander around there. The Principal's Office once used by Mr. Bolte is still an office though now there is a computer in it; I doubt there is still a paddle hanging on the wall, though. The chalkboards still hang on the walls, above which out-of-date maps of the world can still be unrolled from the ceiling, and there are still 1950's vintage ovens in what was once home economics space. It was not familiar territory since we had all of our classes downstairs in the now restricted areas.

In the gymnasium I found that though the tube steel mounting frames still hang down from the gymnasium ceiling; there are no backboards or hoops attached. The original tin backboards are now mounted on the wall; they must have had glass 'boards installed some time after we left. I didn't see the old scoreboard that used a dial-type clock for a timer, either. Like most of the wooden doors I saw, the hardwood floor was warping and cracking and everything had obviously seen its last coat of paint many, many years ago. However, I was able to stand in the spot where Mac hit that miracle whiffle-ball homer.

Whiffle-ball is what we played in the Modale gymnasium for Physical Education on the days it was too rainy to go outdoors. Not quite as fun as dodge-ball but entertaining enough.

We played in our gym shoes or socks. The bases were those orange vinyl squares that didn't grip the varnished hardwood floor very well (at all, actually). The diamond oriented diagonally over the basketball court with home plate at the baseline/sideline corner, first base at the other baseline/sideline corner, second base at the timeline/sideline intersection, and third base at the opposite timeline/sideline intersection. This made game play treacherous. The old stationary wooden bleachers were only four feet outside the court's out of bounds lines so any slip near first or third base would put a person painfully into the front row seats.

If you were to hit a ball onto the elevated stage behind the basketball goal at the far end of the basketball court, it counted as a home run (which didn't happen very often). For as long as I can remember our Phys Ed instructor, Mr. White, said that a ball hit through the basketball hoop at the far end of the court would count as ten runs. Of course swinging harder usually just put more spin on the ball and made them curve into the cheap seats, dive into the floor, or rise up into the ceiling only to fall well short of the hoop and the stage.

Except for the last game we played as 8th graders in 1982.

It was a goof-off game because the school year was about to end, the grades had already been recorded, and we would be off to high school in Mondamin the next fall. I don't remember much about the game except for when Mac dug into the hardwood there at that orange wafer of a home plate. An underhanded pitch was lobbed his way. He let loose with a swing the likes of which I did not see again until the film *The Natural* came out in 1984. It was perfect for the indoor environment: a smooth, easy swing so that there was very little

English on the ball to spin it foul. The trajectory was a low arc that had just enough rise to get the distance for a homer.

And then it happened. The ball had apogeed and was just starting to descend when it hit the front of the rim of the basket and trickled on over through the hoop and net. The one and only ten run homer ever hit at the Modale campus. I'm not sure, but I think Mr. White got a little misty. It was a thing of grade school athletics beauty and a great capper to our elementary school days.

The state of disrepair into which the gym had fallen just didn't do justice to that magnificent feat of whiffleballdom. All in all, it was a very short and sad trip down memory lane. I have to disagree with Thomas Wolfe; you can go home, it just is not the same as when you left.

"It's the Most Wonderful Time of the Year"
The Most Wonderful Time of the Year - Edward Pola and George Wyle

The most Halloween trick-or-treaters ever to stop at our house in Lawrence, Kansas is eleven. All of them received treats so we had no tricks. It was not always so when I was a little kid in Modale.

Dad and Grandpa used to tell me stories about pranksters tipping over outhouses on Halloween, which sounded like a hoot. Except there weren't any outhouses left when I was a teenager.

I recall the railroad crossing lights running most of Halloween night triggered by a 55-gallon barrel being placed across the rails. Toilet paper was always draped over trees all over town.

On All Saints Day most car windows would have soap scribblings on them. A bar of Ivory costs just a few cents and works very well for writing temporary insults on glass. Soap is easily removed with water, natch. However, paraffin would be substituted for the soap if the prankster was feeling particularly vindictive as it requires much more effort to clear.

Shaving cream would be sprayed everywhere. Shaving cream was a tricky prank because it would damage a car's paint so you either had to be über careful and only put it on glass or just really not like the person whose car you were "detailing."

However, my favorite was the launching of all remaining 4th of July fireworks. My friend, Morrow, was great at this because he was always able to come up with M-80's that were much better than the Black Cats, Thunderbombs, and bottle rockets I had managed to save. Nothing says Halloween like the concussion made by an exploding M-80 just after the Witching Hour.

For several years in the early '70's the Modale Legion Hall would be open for a post trick-or-treat get-together. It would be the last stop for the parents and their kids after going door-to-door begging for freebie candy. There was punch, cookies, inedible popcorn balls, and the like. Best of all, "scary" movies like *The Man Called Flintstone* or *The Ghost and Mr. Chicken* would be shown using a 16mm projector and a six foot portable movie screen for all of us costumed little kids sitting on the dirty white vinyl tile floor while the parents milled around talking crop reports and small town gossip (this was when most of the car windows got soaped or shaving creamed).

At our elementary schools in Modale and Pisgah even Mrs. S. would get into the spirit of the season and had us all singing Halloween carols (Christmas carols with "scary" lyrics) in music class.

The scariest Halloween didn't even involve the supernatural unless you consider Orson, Iowa a ghost town.

It's been several years since I've been through Orson (Population 10) or driven past the two houses and abandoned schoolhouse that makes up that ...village.

I used to take my motorcycle through there a lot in junior high when riding up to Pisgah (avoiding all paved roads which the Sheriff and State Patrol might be on) and to visit Morrow just north of Orson. My favorite stop was always to say "hi" to Angie and to drop a couple of hints that she ought to dump her boyfriend. This was an exercise in futility.

But, as a select few of my friends know, the most important thing about Orson is that on Halloween in October of 1985 there was still standing corn all around my friend Mark's house. That evening I had managed to attract a large amount of unwanted attention from several local authorities while driving my truck, the Beast, in and around the town of Modale – Juan and Marvo and their dates were with me - and we drove many back roads for several miles very expeditiously in search of sanctuary.

Kids today may think "drifting" is something noisy little foreign cars do while illegally racing the streets of Tokyo. Most farm kids can tell you it's a skill anyone who has ever driven on gravel roads learns at an early age. The back end of the vehicle glides right across the gravel if you hit sharp turns fast enough. You either become good at it or end up in the road ditch often. I drifted the Beast pretty well that night. So did the guy driving the brown Ford Crown Victoria behind me. Drat.

Sanctuary, as it turned out that evening, was just behind Mark's house where there was a single pass combined in the cornfield (turned out the corn was still too wet to harvest) that allowed me to drive the Beast into the middle of the field and remain out of site of all interested parties who may or may not have been driving behind me using a spotlight to look for that "blue and white Blazer leaving Modale at a high rate of speed."

We all agreed that evening to allow Mark to drive us all home until the unwanted attention lessened. Orson: not just a fading ghost town, it's a veritable safe haven to wayward highwaymen.

Despite having to hide my truck in Orson, Halloween has always been and will always be my favorite time of year. Boo.

"Oh boy, the world can see"
Oh Boy – Buddy Holly

My job is working with airports. I could claim that I have a really complicated job wrought with responsibility but the short of it is I work with airports. Considering my upbringing it was almost a forgone conclusion that somehow my livelihood would involve aviation. What with Grandpa being an Army Air Corps veteran and unlicensed pilot, Dad's addiction to whirlybirds, my watching men hop around on the moon when I was two years old, and the numerous times I went to fly-ins with my family, airfields are in my blood. So, now I work with airports, both large and small.

It was while talking with the manager of a municipal airport not long ago that I was reminded of a story from around 7th grade. This airport manager was planning a fly-in breakfast much like one that I went to one summer day in 1980 or so. A fly-in breakfast is when an airport has an open house inviting anyone with an airplane to, get this, *fly-in* to the airport for breakfast. The residents from town are also invited to attend. This familiarizes the pilots with the location of said airport so they know of one more place to stop for fuel (fuel sales provide much needed revenue to airports) and also demonstrates to the local population how important the airport is to both aviation and to the community.

I believe the fly-in I'm remembering was in Cherokee, Iowa. My uncle, Bob, thought it would be fun to attend, so he asked my dad if he and I would want to go; we agreed. Bob is also my classmate Morrow's uncle and since Morrow and I are friends (and, I guess cousins in a round about way) Bob asked him to come with. And, Bob bumped into an acquaintance, Lyle, one day and, for the hell of it, asked him to ride along, too.

Bob owned a Beechcraft Bonanza, sometimes called the Doctor Killer. This is the same model of aircraft that Roger Peterson, J.P. Richardson, Richie Valens, and Buddy Holly were aboard when they crashed into that Clear Lake cornfield in 1959. It is said to seat five – and, technically speaking, it does - but it's not a roomy fit.

It was about 100 miles as the Bonanza flies which is about thirty to fifty minutes in the air depending on how faded the town names on the water towers are (this was how one navigated the airways before GPS came into being, circling the aircraft around water towers to the name of the town you were over).

We departed the Missouri Valley International Airport early that day. The sky was clear and the temperature cool for the season; a great day to fly. In the crisp morning air the Bonanza leapt off the deteriorating grass-phalt runway and we easily cleared the power lines at the edge of the airfield.

Because the weather was clear the water towers were easy to read allowing us to make the trip in about forty minutes. There were dozens of airplanes there, as well as model aircraft, clowns, and pancakes. A special pancake caterer was there making flapjacks by the hundreds, flipping them through the air in every way imaginable, including handing plates to us kids to use to catch them as they were flipped dozens of feet away from the grill - sorta like a high-carb version of a Japanese grill.

For a couple of hours we looked at all the planes, ate a lot of pancakes, and bought some fuel. Then it was time to depart for Mo. Valley. It wasn't long after take-off that it became very apparent that although it was still a clear and mostly windless day, it wasn't all that cool any more. Quite warm, actually. And, the sun's rays were magnified by the Plexiglas windows of the plane's cabin. The warmth also created some thermal disruptions in the atmosphere that made the ride in the small plane turbulent. To synopsize: cramped, hot, bumpy, and full of pancakes and orange juice.

This didn't bother my dad and Bob in the front bucket seats. Morrow, Lyle, and I in the rear bench seat, however, were a bit uncomfortable. Because of the conditions it seemed like the flight was lasting for hours. But, it was only fifteen minutes or so before the jostling in the hot, stagnant cabin took its toll.

Lyle succumbed to the conditions first and tossed his breakfast. He was neat about it, though. Being a resourceful farmer, he had come prepared - not so prepared to have taken Dramamine - but prepared with a makeshift airsick bag. He may have spared the upholstery from spewage but his choice of receptacles was poor: a large, clear, zip-lock baggie. I think it was one of the half-gallon ones. Morrow and I probably could have survived him getting ill all right but for the fact that we had to see his semi-digested pancakes, toast, and orange juice sloshing around in that clear zip-lock.

A few minutes after Lyle blew chow, Morrow followed suit. The bag now just over half full of breakfasts, I topped off the bag by hurling the remnants of my breakfast. Shortly after I carefully resealed the bag (this was years before "Blue and Yellow Make Green") we touched down at MoValley International. Bob and Dad bounded out of the plane like aces returning from a sortie. Lyle, Morrow, and I staggered out like prom party survivors. We quickly regained our color and some of our dignity after being in the fresh air.

I can't speak for Morrow and Lyle, but it would be several years before I could fly on a small plane without feeling queasy - and it has only been very recently that I can eat a pancake at all. Despite this unfortunate aeronautical event in my formative years I still kept close ties to the General Aviation community. But, it was decades before I was able to make myself attend to another fly-in breakfast.

"Video Killed the Radio Stars"
Video Killed the Radio Stars – The Buggles

When you grow up in a rural farm community where cable television doesn't exist and you are a slave to the crud the three original networks spew or the pomposity of the public television fundraisers, radio plays a huge role in entertaining you.

Before electronic tuning you either had to turn a tuning knob or rely upon a manual push-button to launch the little orange indicator bar to somewhere reasonably near the radio station you wanted to hear.

Stations I remember having buttons set to bring in while in Harrison County ranged widely in style and programming. Dave Wingert on 99.9 KGOR played the light "rock". A character named the Big Guy played "Mickey" for three straight hours on the pop and roll station KQKQ "Sweet" 98.5. 1110 KFAB on the AM dial gave us the time and temperature every 10 minutes. My best friend, Mac, and I listened to oldies on the Mighty 1290 KOIL while working on the county brush crew because those vehicles only had AM radios (the ones that even had radios – not all did). 590 WOW seemed to change formats annually but they were usually good for the farm report.

But what will always be, in my mind, THE station to listen blaring out of the one blown speaker of the truck known affectionately as "the Beast" was 92.3 KEZO. Z-92, the Rock, played the "greatest" music ever made by the likes of Quiet Riot, Def Leppard, REO Speedwagon, the Scorpions, and Bon Jovi. In retrospect, that noise kinda sucks but I was just a stoopid kid so what the hell did I know? Besides, the best aspect of Z-92 - the Rock (I still can't say the first part without thinking the second) wasn't the music; it was the morning team of Otis XII and Diver Dan Doomey. Space Commander Wack, Lance Stallion - Radio Detective, and the Mean Farmer: classic characters created by Otis and Dan, were rivaled only by the immortal (and syndicated) Chicken Man.

And, I will never forget that it was Otis and Dan who proclaimed on the Z-92 airwaves one Monday morning in the summer of 1985 after playing a charity softball game in Pisgah that they had found heaven and it was a potent potables establishment called Ab's Place in River Sioux, Iowa. Having frequented Ab's once or twice myself, I think it is (was) a close second to Mondamin's bar and grill, the Office, but I will defer to the radio personalities' professional judgment.

"That's Entertainment"
That's Entertainment - Arthur Schwartz

Our high school years were a magical time. The cold war was drawing to a close. A computer in each and every home was becoming a reality. Disco had died. And, Professional Wresting was back - with a vengeance.

The A.W.A. (American Wrestling Association) used to be relegated to Sunday morning television along with the reruns of *Hopalong Cassiday, The Lone Ranger,* and *The Cisco Kid.* I used to get up early just to see my favorites: Greg Gagne and Jumpin' Jim Bronzel (the High Flyers), Bobby the Brain Heanon, Baron "the Claw" Von Rasche, the hated Cowboy Bill Watts and Cowboy Bob Ellis, Harley Race, and that strange little man, Joe Swyback, who was always trying to get me to buy some miracle elixir called Gerispeed. But, when Vince McMahon stepped out of the ring, started buying up all those regional wrestling leagues, and morphed them all into the World Wrestling Federation, it was all prime time.

Almost all but a few wrestlers of the mostly mid-west AWA wrestlers were retired. Bobby the Brain, Jesse the Body, the ring announcer Gene Okurland, and Andre the Giant, however, managed to continue their careers on into the 80's.

The Pay-Per-View television spectacle called Wrestlemania was the pinnacle of, well, wrestling mania. Of course, living where we lived in the rural land of no cable television, PPV was almost nonexistent. Besides, there was no way we were going to pay that much to watch wrestling on television anyway.

However, when the WWF came to the Civic Auditorium in Omaha in 1985, my friends Mac, Don Juan, Ford, and I paid our good cash money to go see Jake the Snake, Jimmy Valentine and the Heart brothers, the Iron Sheik, and, the biggest of big, Andre the Giant.

Wow, what a magnificent letdown that turned out to be.

First of all, the fine print on the tickets microscopically warned us that the scheduled matches on the card could be changed without notice – and, naturally, they were: no Andre. Secondly, the wrestlers who were supposed to be hated enemies were easily seen ringside talking before and after the matches like good buddies, and, lastly, what looks somewhat fake on television looks completely, totally, and unabashedly fake live - the microphone UNDER the mat to amplify the body slams and suplexes made it seem – and you wouldn't think this is possible - even more staged.

The most excitement of the whole night was when Ford was driving us home in his folks' powder blue Chevette. We had a carload of young ladies pass us on Interstate 29 and throw a beer bottle at our car that nearly broke out the windshield. That was not fake. I guess we shouldn't have tried to get their attention.

When pro-wrestler "Dr. D" David Schultz smacked reporter John Stossel upside the noggin on ABC television's news show, *20/20*, causing Stossel to permanently lose part of his hearing, it proved that the "sport" could be physically dangerous. None the less for us, any doubt that Rasslin' ain't real was totally erased that night.

Still, we confirmed for ourselves that night (and now it isn't even denied by the participants) that the whole thing is fake. And, even when seen live, it's just not very good, either.

"Fat, Drunk, and Stupid is No Way to Go Through Life"
Dean Wormer speaking to Flounder in the movie *Animal House*

Our high school guidance counselor once told me Scotch whisky is an acquired taste (I believe him to be correct). I believe coffee is, as well.

I first started really drinking coffee late one night the spring of 1986. I was pulling my first all-nighter (for academic purposes), trying to write a twenty-five-page term paper for Mrs. Perley's college preparatory Literature class. I had chosen to quantify my beliefs on how to develop a utopian society in 25 pages and was having trouble. It took Hilton 240 pages in "Lost Horizon" (one of my references) to flesh it out but I was struggling for 25. Jerk.

So, that night I made my first ever pot of coffee. What a wretched decanter of used oil-like sludge that was. But, I drank it because I knew from watching stakeouts on television cop shows that that was how you stayed awake. I don't recall much about what I wrote that night but I do remember drinking my first three pots of coffee (with copious amounts of sugar) and being distracted for a couple of hours by what was the most bizarre thing I had ever seen on television.

I had turned on the television for some background noise but after 2 a.m. channels 3, 6, and 7 out of Omaha had signed off (by playing the National Anthem while showing a waving United States flag). Channel 12 (PBS) had already been off for hours. But, Channel 9 out of Sioux City was still on. It was really fuzzy but that was good since I just wanted some noise to keep me awake but nothing to take away my complete attention.

I don't know what time it was when I realized what was being broadcast on Channel 9; 3ish I'm guessing. I was about two-thirds done with my content when I heard from the television Dean Vernon Wormer say "Put Neidermeyer on it. He's a sneaky little shit just like you." A network station in the rural Heartland dropping an S-bomb like that naturally caught my attention. They were airing *Animal House* and apparently they had missed bleeping that expletive. I pushed aside Utopia to watch the antics of the Deltas. Bluto climbed a ladder to peek in on the sorority girls and, I'll be darned, not only did Channel 9 not bleep out the S-bomb, but they also forgot to cut out the topless pillow fight and Mandy Pepperidge undressing. My interest was, to say the least, piqued.

For whatever reason, Channel 9 was broadcasting *Animal House* unedited and without commercials and, since we didn't have cable or a satellite dish, I was gonna watch this fuzzy presentation - Utopia would just have to wait.

It was near 4:30 a.m. before the final "Ask for Babs" crawled across the screen at the end of the credits before I got back to the paper. I never heard if anyone besides me even knew what Channel 9 had done but I sure appreciated it. I managed to finish the paper and my girlfriend kindly typed it for me. The margins were tweaked and the spacing fudged a bit but I got my 25 pages. *Animal House* is still one of my favorite movie comedies and I now drink at least a half pot of coffee every day - and I have Mrs. Perley to thank for both.

"No! It is I who fooled you! For I am dead... and merely acting alive!"
Master Thespian (John Lovitz) on the television show *Saturday Night Live*

The more I listen to parents here in the "big" city talk of the *one* sport their child plays or the single club at which their kid spends every last waking second the more I appreciate my days at West Harrison.

I had no business starting a varsity basketball game, was not nearly fast enough to run the 440 yard "dash" at the Bob Evans Relays, and certainly didn't have the velocity to pitch relief in a conference baseball game. But, I sure enjoy telling stories about doing all of those, especially since they seem to get better as I get older.

It wasn't just sports I lucked into, there were other activities as well. Maybe at a larger school I would have made the cut for some things. Maybe. But, happily, I will never know.

Take acting, for instance. I have the on-stage presence and enthusiasm of Steven Wright on Quaaludes. And, yet, I was able to land a speaking role in seven of the eight productions done during my high school days. Just call me Master Thespian.

The plays themselves were usually marginal, partly due to wooden performances such as mine, partly due to fossilized subject matter. So as to not offend village sensibilities, the plays Mr. Smith chose were a bit...dated. "Onions in the Stew," "Paint the Town Pink," "We Shook the Family Tree," "Our Miss Brooks." Those were all old plays in the 60's; in the mid 80's they were practically foreign. Only our second to last play, "The Diary of Anne Frank," transcended time.

The truth, for me anyway, was the performance was the worst part of being in a play. Not because it was done live in front of a live audience comprised of dozens of friends and family; hell, I made an ass of myself in front of more people than that without the benefit of a stage and microphone. It was just that the practices were more fun.

People who were a part of the plays back in the day know of what I speak. At each practice some crucial cast member would assuredly be absent due to some extracurricular conflict, requiring one of the other cast members to do double duty at practice and stand-in. My best performances were during those practices where I was hamming it up in someone else's role.

A great deal of gossip was traded backstage while we were waiting for our characters to be needed in a scene. Particularly juicy gossip could cause one to miss his or her cue, especially if the dirt had to do with who was stepping out on whom. Oh, if only they knew what people were saying...

I spent a lot of time looking for places on the set to hide my lines. As much fun as I had playing other people's parts during practice, I never seemed to be able to learn my own. In "The Stuck Pot" I had two pages of the script taped to the back of my prop brief case for a scene I could never quite remember.

As I mentioned before, "The Diary of Anne Frank" was a different production. The stage was more elaborate, using new background "flats" that Mr. Peterson's Shop class had built. An elevated platform and stairway was needed so Mark Shelton and I built that from scrap 2-by material and plywood that may or may not have been swiped from the Shop class. The cast and crew was larger than usual and included students who had previously avoided extracurricular activities (this was most evident during the first performance when the spotlight operator abandoned his post and an entire scene was done in complete darkness and confused the hell out of the audience). As the Frank patriarch I got to swear on stage that, oddly, Mr. Smith thought might be a problem for me. Evidently he never heard the string of expletives I dropped when I fu-... er messed up a line.

A little known and obscure detail to this play, though, was one that I find most memorable. John, one of my closest friends since we met on our first day of kindergarten in late August of 1973, was in "Diary;" only his second high school play. His character, Hans, was a smoker, which is ironic in ways I'm not going to elaborate. As if the stress of trying to not be captured by murderous bigots wasn't enough, Hans had to constantly bitch and moan about not having any cigarettes. In one scene, though, a cig, albeit an old, dried out one, was procured for him, and he eagerly lights up. The cigarette is supposed to flare because it is so dry. John took it as a personal challenge to create a prop cigarette (two actually, because for the first time in school history we did the play two nights) that would flare when lit. Using a little farm-kid know-how - and a fair amount of gunpowder from a Black Cat firecracker left over from Halloween - John rigged up a couple of special fake smokes. But only two. There weren't enough materials - so he said - for testing.

So, the night of the first show, things go, well, like the first night of a high school play. The curtains didn't get pulled at the end of a scene. As I said before, another scene is done in complete darkness for want of a spotlight operator (Tracy, where the hell were you?), despite

72

years of practice I stumbled over the word "damn," and then it came time for John/Hans to light up.

"Oh, Miep! Cigarettes!" The match was stroked across the strip of sandpaper as if in the hands of a seasoned veteran (he must have rehearsed this a great deal outside of play practice). There was a hiss and crackle of the flame as the matchstick was raised to the end of the faux cigarette. The cast stared at John's hands as he put the flame to the frail paper prop. He inhaled and the cigarette tip glowed, probably due to the small amount of cigarette tobacco that was in front of the gunpowder. Then POOF. Son of a bitch if it didn't work perfectly. Fortunately no one heard the perfectly enunciated "damn" of admiration I said when John's prop smoke filled the air. Genius.

The second night went better in most respects, although John's second - and last - prop cigarette did hesitate before flaring brilliantly, causing us all to panic ever so briefly. And, just like the abbreviated flare of John's cigarettes, that production ended. There was one more play before we graduated but it paled in comparison to "Diary."

I almost forgot: anyone who was part of play in those days knows the best part was the cookies. Mrs. Smith's chocolate chip cookies were often brought to play practice and were a staple at ever post-production cast party. Forty excruciating minutes on stage was worth it to get one of those cookies.

"All right, Mr. DeMille, I'm ready for my close-up"
Norma Desmond in the movie *Sunset Blvd.*

I never used to watch the Oscars when I was growing up. Although I watched hundreds of movies on the ol' TV during my formative years, the Academy always seemed to award actors who meant little to me playing roles for which I had no interest in films I never saw.

Well, in many ways that hasn't changed. I haven't seen any of this year's nominated films although I will rent several of them once they are issued on DVD so's I can watch them at home where there are no laser pointers dotting the screen and the popcorn and sodas don't require a second mortgage on the house to acquire.

Watching a montage of previous Best Film winners, I find that I have, in fact, seen several award winners, just years (decades in many cases) after their release. I didn't develop an interest in the classic greats until 1985 when my best friend, Mac, introduced my buddies Ford, Don Juan, and me to the Summer Film Series at the University of Nebraska - Omaha.

We saw several that summer, including these greats: *A Boy and His Dog* (Winner of a Hugo in 1976 for Best Dramatic Presentation) starring a young Don Johnson wandering a post-apocalyptic world with his telepathic dog.

Repo Man (Winner of a 1985 Saturn Award from the Academy of Science Fiction, Fantasy & Horror Films for Best Supporting Actor - Tracey Walter) starring Emilio Esteves as an apprentice repossession agent who stumbles onto a UFO cover-up years before Mulder and Scully.

And, the greatest work of art we saw that summer, *Monty Python and the Holy Grail* (Nominated for a Hugo in 1976 for Best Dramatic Presentation) the documentary about King Arthur's search for the Holy Grail.

All were masterpieces of their genres. Besides never forgetting seeing these fine films for the first time on the medium screen in one of UNO's auditoriums, the other thing I will never forget is the pre-movie supper we had prior to seeing *Repo Man.*

We got to campus too early and decided to grab something to eat before the movie started. Eating choices for high schoolers on a limited budget are slim in that area of Omaha. We ended up at the Burger King on Dodge Street east of campus, somewhere in the 35th

Street area. Like all Burger Kings, the food was quite unremarkable. The clientele and ambiance, however, were unforgettable.

There was an extremely intoxicated and presumably homeless gentleman (no, not me) in the BK that night, and he was stumbling, bumbling around, blabbering incoherently, and generally making a scene. No, it wasn't our classmate, Bobby, either.

We were transfixed by the show before the show; the rowdiness increased for no obvious reason other than substance abuse. The climax was when the drunk toppled to the floor in a heap. The conclusion was when he lost control of his bodily functions; self-defecating humor, as it were. With a vile stench starting to waft through the King we decided to exit [stage right] and head back to UNO to watch the movie. Both shows made us laugh hysterically. I still like the movie *Repo Man* but I don't eat at Burger King as much as I did during my high school freshman through junior years.

"What a waste of machinery"
Spoken to Toad in the movie *American Graffiti*

Contrary to common sense, one could cruise Mondamin. The loop started at the Slab and went straight east down Highway 127/183 to a smaller version of the Slab in front of the last house at the east edge of town - exactly one mile - flip a U-ee, and return to the Slab.

On a busy night, say after a basketball game, there could be nearly twenty trucks and cars on the loop at once - eight four-wheel-drive Chevy pick-ups, seven four-wheel-drive Ford pick-ups, one '72 Mustang, two Camaros, and two Novas (one a classic muscle car and the other the anemic econo-box model that the bastards at Chevrolet built in the early '80's). Only a handful of these vehicles would be new enough to still retain their original color, the rest are varying shades of rust and primer; mostly hand-me-downs from the family farm but suitable for a teen-aged driver. Most would have "customized" exhaust systems that may or may not include a muffler, rumbling with gas guzzling growls that easily advanced us decades closer to a total ice cap thawing. I'm pretty sure my truck, the Beast, single-handedly started the hole in the ozone layer. With such a short loop and so few cruisers there was a certain familiarity developed; whenever I saw a green Ford F-150 approaching I would go British and drive in the left lane. The Ford would do the same. It was an understanding we had and both of us were too scared to be the first to quit doing that.

Cruising Mondamin was just like *American Graffiti* except the strip was shorter, there were no traffic signals, there weren't as many cars, and the cars weren't as nice. And, sometimes the loop was snow packed. Oh, and there was no young Suzanne Sommers in a white T-bird, either. Other than that, it was just like cruising in the movies.

Although shooting the loop with three or four other cars in a town of 400 where not even the gas station stayed open past 5pm may sound like the pinnacle of weekend excitement, truth be told, Missouri Valley is where cruising on Friday and Saturday nights usually happened.

When I was really little sometimes the family would stop by the Dairy Den in the Valley for soft serve ice cream (chocolate-vanilla swirl in a sugar cone for me, in a paper cup for my accident-prone sister). The Dairy Den is just a small shack about twenty feet wide and thirty feet long. Since there's no seating, you order at one of the three windows at the front of the building and then eat in your car.

As good as the ice cream was, the best part of these family outings was backing into one of the six unmarked parking spots around the little brown treat hut and watching the cars cruising the loop. Ideally located near the west edge of the businesses on the south side of Erie Street (which is also U.S. Highway 30 as it passes through town) and with a half gravel -half asphalt circle driveway, the Dairy Den was at the west end of the Mo Valley loop. Option One of the west end, actually. The gas station one block west on Blaine Street was Option Two.

We would watch for half an hour or so as sedans, pick-ups, econo-boxes, station wagons, and even an occasional sports car bounced over the pot-hole filled driveway as they changed directions and turned to head east back down Erie to cruise back to the east side of the Valley. Every once and awhile a rusted out POS (Piece of Stuff) would stomp on the accelerator and spin one rear tire for a few feet. The sports cars, however, almost never did that; usually they did just the opposite and stealthily eased back into traffic. Dad told me it's because when you've got it you don't have to show off. Still, every once and awhile, there would be a Camaro/Trans Am, Mustang/Thunderbird, Monte Carlo/Cutlass/Regal, or classic Nova that would drop the hammer and get a posi-traction second gear scratch. Then the trip around the loop began.

Heading east on Erie from the Dairy Den starts with five blocks of houses on the left and houses on the right, some with people sitting on the porches watching the automotive spectacle. Then, where Highway 183 (1st Street) from Mondamin and other northern locations links up with Highway 30 (Erie) was the Li'l Duffer, Mo Valley's "fast" food place. The Duffer had a huge parking lot that was a good place to park your car if you were meeting someone or to pull in for a chat. And, if you were desperate, you could even eat the food there.

Three blocks further to the east, past a couple of banks, the Breadeaux Pizza Shoppe, and the closed Rialto movie theater, was the most important part of the loop, the ancient, three story, brick City Hall/Fire Station/Police Station/City Jail building. When nothing is happening, there would be three police cars parked next to the building. A typical night would have just two police cars parked. On busy nights there was only one parked; none would be there during a crisis or the county fair. It was important to make a count on your first trip around the loop so you would know how many of the Men in Blue were out patrolling.

There was one summer night that Al and I brought a bunch of water balloons with us and chucked them at people walking on the sidewalks. We didn't count the police cars and didn't realize there was more than one officer patrolling so it wasn't long before the one cop we hadn't kept track of pulled us over (right after we tossed our final barrage of balloons) and issued us a stern warning for unlawful use of dihydrogen monoxide. We never did that again.

Then came the lone traffic light. If you kept your speed at a constant 30 miles per hour the light would be green every pass (or red every pass if you were out of synch). Another couple of blocks and Highway 183 breaks off and heads south to Council Bluffs. Just two more blocks and the east end of the loop is reached.

Turn left across Erie, hit the 8th Street entrance to the Kum 'n' Go, bounce across their busted up concrete, and exit through their Erie Street driveway and the flip is complete, now traveling west on Erie. Like the Dairy Den at the other end of the loop, the Kum 'n' Go gas station is the most convenient place to change direction.

Further east was another ice cream shop, Al's Dairy Sweet, which also had the soft serve ice cream and cute girls taking orders but the mystery meat burgers weren't as tasty as the Dairy Den loose meats. A Pizza Hut was out that direction, too, but its steep driveway was not conducive to turning around. Even further east was the Sunnyside Inn Truck stop but that was too remote to be in the loop.

Many summer (and spring, fall, and winter) nights were spent driving the Mo Valley loop, radio tuned to Z-92 the Rock (92.3 on your FM dial) with Def Leppard blaring through the lone in-dash speaker of the Beast, windows down, usually with a truck full of friends, sometimes a girlfriend, sometimes alone, honking and yelling at other people on the loop, who were also driving the vehicular grapevine hoping to hear of something to do.

I was with my neighbor, Matt, one night in his grandpa's '84 metallic blue Ford pickup (only 2 wheel drive) and he threw my baseball uniform hat out the window into the center of Erie Street. Ha, ha, very freakin' funny. The car behind us did its best to swerve and run over it but missed. Everyone else on the circuit got it, though, including Matt on the return trip; the hat was a total loss. Such was the entertainment on the loop.

If you were lucky you find someone on their way to a party (there were parties every weekend but if you didn't know to which cornfield or timber to go you'd never find one) or hook up with another group of bored people on their way to Council Bluffs or Omaha to see a movie.

Or, sometimes just cruise until it was as empty as the Mondamin loop and go home.

I still make a lap around the loop when I go back home just to see how it's changed. There are two more traffic lights which really screws up the timing, the Li'l Duffer is now some pizza place, the Rialto shows movies again, Breadeaux Pizza (better than the Hut) is gone, and there's a Casey's General Store at 1st and Erie. But, with all the new fast food places out by the intersection of Highway 30 and Interstate 29 outside of the west end of town it doesn't seem like there's as many kids cruising. Or, maybe I'm just old.

"If you won't race, you can't win."
From *Chariots of Fire*

A few years ago I crossed off another dubious achievement from my list of stuff I might do sometime in my life if I can't come up with an excuse fast enough. I ran a 5K in the Kansas City Corporate Challenge, a metro area wide Olympics of sorts pitting area businesses against one another. Still remaining on my list is "Training to run a 5K." It wasn't really by choice: some (former) friends convinced me our team needed the [single inconsequential] event participation point for someone of my advanced maturity. Never again will I believe them when they say, "it's not really that far." Stoopid metric system.

The day after my ill-advised participation in a 5K I only felt marginally worse. It wasn't so much the ice-pick jabs in my right hip or the quad muscles in my legs that felt like a seven day clock with a nine day wind as it was the achilles tendons that felt as tight as the string on the bow used to launch the arrow that dropped, well, Achilles. But, it was the shins that felt as though they had been smacked with a five-pound mallet that reminded me of home.

The throbbing pain made me remember track practice, both at Modale in Junior High, and in Mondamin during High School. There was no such thing as "Cross Country" in those early years of the 1980s and yet that's how we trained for track for six years, just like the classes twenty years before us and the other classes for another three after we graduated.

Our high school training facilities, such that they were, were vastly superior to our junior high experience. Our first two years in High School track were spent practicing by running on the pothole filled street in front of our school bus barn for short sprints and hurdles, running out into the country along Kelly Lane west of town for distance training. When we were juniors the Guttau family was kind enough to let us run laps in their horse pasture that was just outside of town, about a mile from the school. A regular oval; a 440-yard oval. With horse stuff every so often, but, hey, we just learned a few years earlier than most that life is a lot of running in circles and is littered with horse crap.

The Modale Junior High practice was done by running along the edge of the school building, past the merry-go-round, take a left at the teeter-totters, onward by the basketball goal, around the big tree (also used as home plate for the small kick-ball field), along the fence by the creek, another left at the fence corner post, behind the big kick-

81

ball field backstop, north along the sidewalk, one more turn at the monkey bars, skirt the swing set, and one last turn to the right and there's one lap. One 300-yard lap. One not-quite-a-quarter-mile lap with a buttload of turns. Why, everyone knows that a 440 is one and five-twelfths of a lap with two right turns and four left ones. Yet, we never won a track meet. Go figure.

But, we did win an occasional event. When one of my (ex)friends talked me into participating in that Corporate Challenge track meet last year it really meant only one thing: downing a couple dozen ibuprofen the next day. Having not wised-up in the least since that 5K fiasco, I agreed to play a minimal role. Fools. I was entered into the 400 meter "dash." Dash? What the hell? I couldn't dash that far 20 years ago, and I still ain't dashing it now.

But, back in the day, when we were in junior high, there was a time when I rode on the coattails of my classmate, Earl. Earl moved to Mondamin right at the start of the BMX craze and his dad opened a bicycle shop called "Yuck, Muck, and Duck's." In addition to being a pretty darned good bicycle rider, Earl was a damned fast runner. About a 57 second 440. Yards, that is. Remember yards? That's what we ran then, back when kids were still expected to learn math and could understand multiples of numbers that aren't rounded to the nearest 100. 220, 440, 880, the – gasp - Mile and the – heaven forbid - 2 Mile; I swear, in addition to the moral decay of society in general, the metric system is creating a whole generation of mathematically stunted morons.

But, I digress.

Anyhoo, Earl was one quick son of a Yuck. No matter how far behind I got us in the Mile (that's 1760 yards) Relay, Earl always managed make up most if not all of the ground and get us a medal. My track career suffered considerably when he and his family moved up north to Onawa. At least the weather at my most recent track experience was warm. Those stoopid Bob Evans Relays (the Logan-Magnolia Track, not the restaurant) in early spring always seemed to be an overcast, drizzly, chilly affair. Unfortunately, I'm still too slow and I have no idea where Earl is so, no medals for me anymore.

It was just a few days after "dashing" a 440 at a snail's pace, swearing my track career was done, that I ended up substituting as the 880-yard leg (800 meters for you metric types) of a distance medley. This really verified that much like I haven't managed to mature appreciably over the last twenty-five years, I haven't gotten any more fleet of foot, either. Slowed down quite a bit, actually. As I was gasping for oxygen with still a lap of my leg remaining, I began hallucinating back to 1981 when I went with my girlfriend, Alisa, and her family down to Omaha to the Westroads theaters to see an incredibly boring film called *Chariots of Fire*. I never imagined I would ever reenact a portion of that movie but that night I did.

For those last 440 yards of my half-mile I was living that classic scene from the film where the group of Brits, dressed in the old school white running togs, were running on the West Sands beach. Not so much because I was in a group, no, the group was quite a ways ahead of me. Not because any of us were Brits, either, because, well 'cause this is the land of red necks, not red coats. Nor was it because I was wearing white; I had on the black and silver just like my days at West Harrison. And, I wasn't anywhere near a beach.

Nope, the part of that scene that I reenacted as the movie's instrumental theme played through my head was the sssllllloooowww mmmmoooooottttttiiiiioooonnnn that apparently only I - and the really slow chump behind me - were running. As I cruised to a new personal worst of a three minute 880, I reminded myself of those guys on the state qualifying 2 mile relay team back in 1984 (Nut, Al, Neal, and T.R.) were undefeated that season because their 880's were in the 2 minute range. It was cool then but I appreciate the speed of it a lot more now. Nothing slaps as hard – not even a very disinterested woman at the Beamer's Nightclub in Ames – as the realization that those days were the best and it all gets slower from there. Damn.

The only good thing about my adult track experience was being able to just leave the stadium, jump in my own car, and drive myself home. No waiting for the rest of the team, no buses, and most importantly, no pranks.

One late afternoon in 1984 while track practice was going on and we (the track teams) were running laps around the block just north of the school buildings (Note to young-uns: Like I said before: back in our day we didn't have no stinkin' track for practice and meets; we ran on the streets and liked it that way).

My classmate, Heather, was on the women's track team and was a really good sprinter and hurdler. She was also fairly nice to me and was loads of fun to pick on. While she was doing her laps some miscreants lifted up on the rear bumper of the blue hulk of a car she drove and placed some wood blocks under the back axle so that the tires were imperceptibly just off the ground.

Word of what had been done spread fairly quickly through the track teams and after track practice was over most of us found an excuse to be near her car when she got in it to go home.

She started the engine and threw it into reverse to back out of her parking spot. The wheels turned but the car stood still. People snickered. She gunned the engine and the car still did not move. People started to laugh. She really stood on it and the wheels were doing about 50 but the car remained quite stationary.

She looked up, saw everyone laughing, and flashed a glare of fury at us all that I didn't even know she was capable of making. She slammed the gearshift into park and the tranny made that awful clacking-grinding sound that an automatic transmission makes when it's mercilessly abused in such a manner.

She jumped out of her car and hurled out combinations of expletives never before uttered in the school parking lot (that I had been present to hear, anyway). Since the humor was depleted, a few of us lifted the car up and sheepishly removed the blocks. She was still pissed when she left. In retrospect, that was probably too mean of a joke for such a nice person but damn, it was funny at the time.

But, now I am officially retired. No more track and field for me anymore. Ever. And, this time, I mean it.

"Badgezz? We Don't Need No Steenkeeng Badgezz!"
Mexican Banditos signing up for duty in the movie *Blazing Saddles*

A Taco Bell resides just four blocks from my home in Lawrence, Kansas. This summer, the good folks at PepsiCo decided that my Taco Bell was in such a sad state that it completely demolished the building and rebuilt it in the exact same spot with the same basic footprint, even leaving the same crummy entrance/exit drive virtually unchanged. Seeing this newest version of the Taco Bell architecture made me think of a story.

This story is just that: a story. The location, characters, and plot may sound familiar to you. One of you may even think you witnessed the following event. But, because of the sheer preposterousness of this story, it is an obvious fabrication borne solely of my own imagination.

This bit of fiction is set in the winter of my senior year of high school around State Wrestling Tournament time. Since the main character of this story is a basketball player (this year), his season has mercifully come to its end. But, at this time (1985-1986) we had some pretty talented wrestlers at W-H, which meant their season would not conclude until the State Tourney had run its course. If this were a real story and not just something I've made up, I'd say that a classmate named Bobby was representing us at State that year.

I'd like to say that the fictional hero of this story - I'll call him "Deke" just to simplify the story - was a rabid wrestling fan who wanted to make the trek to Des Moines to cheer on his fictional classmate, Bobby. Indeed, "Deke" was a huge wrestling fan, though it was the WWF he followed and Rowdy Roddy Piper was the rassler for whom he usually cheered, but I digress. The truth was much more self-centered: this was a great excuse to ditch school for a couple of days and maybe even catch a minute or two with the wrestling cheerleader he was dating. Oh, and watch Bobby wrestle.

This story would be quite boring were it only about a single spectator at a high school wrestling tournament. This is not the case. To spice things up a bit, I'll add a few more characters. Because gas at that time was so expensive for poor high school kids (just over a dollar a gallon) I'll say for the sake of the story that "Deke" carpools to Des Moines with another W-H student named - again, for the sake of this story - "Marvo." To add further interest, I'll say that they drive to Des Moines in "Marvo's" green Ford F-150 pick-up along with "Marvo's" girlfriend who shall remain unnamed.

The trip out was benign enough - I mean, would have been if it ever really occurred. The drive was across the state on Interstate 80 East - about two and a half hours at the 55 mph speed limit - accomplished in this story in about an hour and forty-five minutes. As always, the tournament was held at Veteran's Memorial Auditorium, later called "The Barn" when the Iowa Barnstormers Arena Football team played there.

After arriving in record time the trio wandered around the Vet much like the other teenagers from across the state who were also ditching school. Having never been to a State Tournament, "Deke" watched a few matches, talked to Bobby and a couple of the cheerleaders, and subsequently got bored. Even "Marvo" who was a wrestler (and, fictionally, would also be a State qualifier the following year) got bored with watching the matches.

They left early and went to the Drake University campus to beg for temporary lodging from a Drake sophomore who was a West Harrison graduate. I'll call him "Todd." "Todd" lived in a fraternity house, and he not only supplied a floor to sleep upon but also a bottle of a reddish, syrupy looking stuff called Amaretto that mixed quite well with Pepsi – but was not so swell when consumed straight.

"Todd" also was kind enough to take the trio to a little slice of heaven in Des Moines called "Peggy's." Peggy's is a college watering hole near the Drake campus - stumbling distance - that is the size of a shoebox and was staffed by bartenders not overly concerned about the age of its patrons. If this had, in fact, actually occurred, the happenings of this night would be a little hazy. So to preserve the illusion of reality, I won't endeavor to fabricate anything other than to say there were too many inexpensive pitchers of beer drank at Peggy's, too many Amaretto and Pepsi's (and too much straight Amaretto) consumed at the fraternity house. All of this led to prank phone calls to the cheerleader's hotel and later to making an offering to the fraternity's porcelain god.

The next morning all were suffering from severe bouts of brown bottle flu. A squirrel was hopping from limb to limb in the massive oak tree outside the fraternity house, effortlessly rising higher and higher in an almost mocking fashion. In a flash of hangover justice, the fuzzy little tree rat missed a limb on one of its hops, plummeted forty feet to the ground, and hit with a muted "thump." It bounced once after impact and then lay motionless, surely deceased. Wrong! After ten minutes it stirred a bit. Then it arose, moving very slowly and staggered away, much like the inhabitants of the House watching it; however, unlike those suffering the hangovers, it quickly regained its spryness and climbed up the tree back to the branch from which it had fallen.

After having a breakfast of donuts and Pepsi, the trio returned to Vets for the last day of the Tournament. Even though it was the conclusion, non-wrestlers could find it uninteresting as the "Deke" in this story did. The fictional high school wrestler, Bobby, did take 6th place. By late afternoon interest had waned to the point that leaving seemed like a good idea, so they hopped into that green Ford and headed west down University Avenue to leave the metropolis of Des Moines; however, before they hit the open road, they decided to grab a bite to eat. The first place they saw was Taco Bell.

Who's to say how the idea arose? Since this is pure fiction, I'll say that all three had a diabolical epiphany when the truck pulled into that Taco Bell. This was one of the original Taco Bell restaurants, built in the John Wayne movie set Mexican architectural style, complete with a bell. For several years there had been idle speculation on just how cool it would be to have one of those bells, but no one ever appropriated one. Yet. "Marvo" parked his truck in the rear of the parking lot at the back of the building. He backed into the space and pointed the truck towards the exit. Taking the bell had become a virtually unspoken forgone conclusion. It was there; they were there: it had to be time to get one. The farmer's multi-tool (a pair of pliers) and a Crescent wrench were retrieved from the back of the pickup. And, just like that, it was on.

At the back of the 'Bell, there was a big green box that housed an electrical transformer to power the place. There was also a jungle gym-like conglomeration of natural gas lines piped into the building. The transformer and piping were laid out almost as if the designer had intended to create a ladder to reach the roof. They waited for a lone car in the Drive-thru lane to pass and they bolted from the truck to the transformer. They hopped up on it and then jumped over to the gas pipes, which, thankfully, were able to handle the additional load of people climbing them.

Much like the squirrel they had watched earlier in the day, they climbed up the gas pipe ladder and crawled onto the roof. Because this is fiction, this all happened without any other cars passing through the Drive-thru lane to see all this illicit activity – a bit of luck that surely would not have happened in actuality. They crawled across the roof to the peak where it met the façade from which the bell hung.

The first of two disappointments came to light. The stinkin' bell was made of fiberglass! Two feet high and about the same in diameter, it appeared to be a brass beauty, but it was every bit as fake as the rest of the Hispanic theme of the building. One rap with the pliers made that very clear, as a muffled 'thunk' resonated nowhere. At least it would be very light; a brass bell that size would weigh hundreds of pounds.

The next disappointment was how the bell was mounted. A quarter-inch steel bolt ran through the faux eight-inch by eight-inch wood support, through the top of the bell with a washer and nut inside the fiberglass securing the bell. The bell was so narrow at its top that neither the wrench nor the pliers would reach the nut inside. Stymied, "Marvo" leaned against the bell that gave way, nearly allowing him to roll off the front of the roof. He regained his balance; they saw that the bolt bent. It bent quite easily. "Deke" grabbed the bell and pulled it back towards them; the bolt bent again but in the opposite direction. They looked at one another, grinned, and then grabbed the bell and started rocking the bell back and forth, bending the bolt over and over. To the five o'clock rush hour traffic on University Avenue the permanently stationary bell had to appear to be finally tolling.

There was a small bank branch office next door to the Taco Bell. Although it was closed, it looked to be having some sort of party as there were many people inside it eating snacks and drinking punch. A few of the party-goers saw the stealthy ascent to the roof and stood at the window watching the two teens pushing the bell fore and aft of the stucco'd façade.

After a few minutes of effort the weathered bolt snapped and the bell was free. The two scrambled back to the back edge of the roof. "Marvo" jumped to the ground, bypassing the gas pipe ladder. "Deke," the acrophobic, tossed down the bell and carefully climbed down the pipes and gingerly touched ground. He ran like hell to the pick-up in which the bell was tossed, engine started, and rolling slowly. The mouths of the spectators in the bank hung open as "Deke" jumped into the moving truck and slammed the door shut. They departed the parking lot – and the City of Des Moines – at a quick clip but slowly enough to not draw too much official attention.

The two-hour drive back to the safety of Mondamin was spent replaying the details of the coup. By the time they arrived home it was decided that the bell would be stowed in the shed at "Deke's" place. It would make a fine punch bowl at special events.

And, there the bell remained for years until it was taken to a local dump by one of "Deke's" relatives who didn't understand the significance of the prize. And that, my friends and fellow classmates and graduates of West Harrison, is the purely made-up and fictional myth of the abscondsion of a Taco Bell bell.

Taco Bell restaurants no longer have bells – they were all replaced with lighted signs in the late 80's, possibly in response to having heard a story similar to this one. As stated in the preface, to some this may sound familiar; but I assure you that any resemblance to people, places, vehicles, or actions that you believe you may know or have known is purely coincidental. Unless, of course, someone can provide proof that the statute of limitations has run out for said actions...

"So what? So Let's Dance!"
Al Cervic in the movie *Caddyshack*

My wife and I went to see the Harry Potter movie *The Goblet of Fire* and liked it nearly as well as we liked the book. The movie included a school dance which, quite naturally, reminded me of those totally awesome, "kick - a" high school dances we used to have in the high school gymnasium Back Home.

I'm going to ignore the junior high "dances" we used to have at the Modale and Mondamin Legion Halls because those were more like parties since they were usually more groups of rambunctious boys, groups of girls making fun of the rambunctious boys, and a few current "couples" dancing awkwardly to whatever music was coming from the boom box cassette player (or combination turntable/radio/eight track player stereo and speakers if someone really went to some trouble). Although, I should note that at least the junior high dances usually had chips, sodas, and other assorted munchies and were almost always decorated with streamers, balloons, and assorted seasonal accoutrement. I don't recall, other than for prom, decorating the gymnasium very extensively other than with festive "Hawkeye Pride" posters on the walls.

The music at the high school dances was somewhat better: instead of the kid with the biggest cassette tape collection running the boombox, we almost always had Complete Music DJ service ($500 a gig) who had a decent sound system, a really big cassette tape collection, and a few of those new plastic disc thingies that would sometimes skip (a lot like a 45 record would). High school dances also usually were on a Friday night often following a loss at some sporting event. If not for being part of Student Council (the dance sponsor) I probably would have ceded my part of the gym's main entrance doorframe to someone else to lean against to watch the goings-on.

Much like Harry and Ron discovered in the Harry Potter movie, asking someone to the dance was the most excruciatingly difficult task ever known to man in the entire history of the universe. It's especially difficult in a small town environment where you've known everyone your age for your entire life. How you can come across as a cool upperclassman when everyone knows every dumbass thing you've done since birth? I think there were maybe a dozen dances thrown the whole time the Class of '86 was in school and I'm pretty sure I had dates to three of them - and one of those dates asked me. 'Course, it would have helped if I knew how to dance...

"Home, where my thought's escaping"
Homeward Bound – Simon and Garfunkel

Homecoming Week at West Harrison has changed a bit from when I was there over twenty years ago. Some familiar events planned such as Deviation Day on Thursday and Black and White Day on Friday still occur. Even before I was in high school I always looked forward to Skit Night during Homecoming Week? Every class did two skits and, based upon audience response, a "winner" was chosen, almost always done by the Senior Class, although our Junior year we had the spirit trophy in the bag except for being penalized for "tampering" with the Class of '85's props (why the heck did you have to get caught, Bobby?)

The obligatory Pie Eating Contest was great to watch, especially if you knew what extra ingredients had been added to the pies when no one was watching. Why any of the faculty ever agreed to participate still defies explanation.

I have photographs of skit practice we had at the Globe house when we were juniors. In one shot my friend, Missy, is wearing a shower cap but I don't remember why. One of the skits we did was based on that racy game show *Love Connection* that now seems pretty tame when compared to today's *Elimidate* or *Room Raiders*. My good friend, Ford, and I emceed Skit Night '85. Inspired by that new late night talk show guy named Letterman we were decked out in jeans and suit coats, and I wore my baseball hat (I still have that W-H hat somewhere back home). I distinctly remember one joke we did about seeing an Arab roofer on the way to school that day, the punch line being "Shi'ite on a shingle." Twenty-some years later and that lame joke is still topical.

In 1984 we had convinced Principal Penkert that the Homecoming Parade should be resurrected. I don't know what we said to make that happen; maybe I just forged his name onto a memo much like I had done onto so many of my hall passes. But, that year the parade returned. That experience taught me that several things:

1. Kids who've never built a parade float before in their lives can still turn an old hayrack, chicken wire, and hundreds of napkins swiped from Missouri Valley's Li'l Duffer fast food joint into a respectable looking float.
2. Interstate mile marker signs are not for use on parade floats. Ever.
3. Never put Bobby in charge of finding supplies. What he will obtain is even more verboten than mile markers, and

93

4. It is acceptable for Mac to say "kick butt" over the rescue unit PA to a large crowd of people. The crowd will erupt with cheers.

Do they still have the parade? Do they still paint the windows downtown for Spirit Week? Can "kick butt" still be said over a loudspeaker without recrimination? All burning Homecoming questions to which I probably don't really want to know the answers.

Later that Homecoming Friday night in 1984 our football team was poised to pull off an upset victory in our Homecoming game. The weather turned to crap shortly after Mac said, "kick some butt" over the ambulance public address speaker. It had been raining buckets throughout the entire game. Time was winding down in the fourth quarter and we were down 8 to 6.

It was small town, Class 1A football where real men always went for it on 4th down and always went for the two-point conversion after touchdowns; nobody kicked the ball unless all other options had been exhausted. In the interest of full disclosure, most small town high school football teams don't have a capable place kicker.

We had the ball on their 12 yard line and it was 4th and long; we had no choice but to try the unlikely: a field goal. The rain was still coming down in sheets, not quite the perfect storm, but annoying enough. Ford, Superintendent Holland, and I were standing in the end zone, soaked to the bone, watching as Bob, a Senior and the closest thing we ever had to a kicker, lined up for a game winning field goal. Despite the fact that the team never practiced field goal plays and Bob only worked on kicking on his own time, the play was executed perfectly.

Ford, the Sup, and I all threw our arms in the air as we watched Bob's kick arcing along a path that would bisect the space between the uprights. It looked to be a beauty and we were cheering it on, all the way to the goal posts where it passed just *beneath* the cross arm. We stood there silent and dumbfounded, staring at the rain-drenched ball lying there in the end zone grass as time ran out. The Homecoming dance that night was a real bummer.

"And me all starry-eyed "
Only Time Will Tell - Asia

Our high school band and chorus director, Bruce, absolutely abhorred marching band (and pep band, too) but directed it because it was in his contract, got Laura, Morrow, and I into a Southwest Iowa Marching Band that was going to march in the Cotton Bowl Parade in 1985. This marching band was led by Lee Nelson, the band director from the Harlan Community School District (who was an anti-Bruce and reveled in teaching jazz, pep, and marching band). We, along with over 200 other musicians from the southwest quarter of the state gathered in Red Oak a half-dozen times over the summer and fall of 1984, learning to play Dvořák's "New World Symphony" and Asia's "Only Time Will Tell" while marching in unison, with a couple a fancy double time steps thrown in for pizzazz.

My Grandpa Maule drove me to practice a couple of times and I remember him sitting in his red and black Chevrolet S-10 extended cab pick-up truck reading the newspaper or napping while the band (which was two to ten times larger than the individual school bands from which we came) marched all over the burg of Red Oak. For the majority of us, the only time we have ever played those two songs was in Red Oak.

Oops. Correction: most of us only played that song in TWO places: Red Oak and Dallas. Yes, we all said we would diligently practice at home but I never met anyone in the band who would cop to practicing anything ever. Ever. Sure, there were a few über-geeks who did, but most of us did not. The music wasn't that tough and most of the band members were quite good. I remember the drum line being scary-good. The cadence they played still runs through my head whenever I'm walking somewhere. The experience of playing in a band where there are more than one or two of most instruments was indescribable. If you went to a big school you have no idea what I mean. The West Harrison marching band had maybe 20 people in it. I played trumpet parts on my tenor sax because we had too few trumpets to carry the melody. In this band, though, I was one of eight tenor saxophones. Wow, tenor sax parts are boring. We played the same harmony parts the barely-a-tones played. But, nothing sounds better than having all the instruments an arrangement requires playing in-time and in-tune. At full strength the sound was incredible and gave me goose bumps. Just like the Iowa State University Cyclone Football Varsity Marching Band does with their warm-up arpeggios; I am grateful our nephew plays in the ISU band and wish I had.

So, at the end of December in 1984, we all boarded Crusader Coach Lines buses (my bus was driven by friend and parent of classmates, Duane Grooms) and headed south to the Big D and I don't mean divorce. The Cotton Bowl game itself was to be between Boston College and the University of Houston. We all knew Boston College because of the pass that had been replayed ad-nauseum leading up to New Year's Day. The highlight of the trip occurred at our New Year's Eve mixer in the hotel's banquet room when Doug Flutie himself stopped by and waved 'hello' to us. Turned out he was staying at our hotel, too, to get away from the press.

The low light was the parade itself. An unusual weather phenomenon caused the temperature to drop below freezing. That would have been no big deal in Iowa where we had all left our cold weather gear but in Texas where it should have been much warmer it sucked big time. I remember my thumb going numb before the parade even started because I had no gloves and the thumb rest on my sax was frozen brass. And, the parade route that appears to be miles long on the TV was actually only a few blocks long, some of which was in a neighborhood that seemed a bit seedy. Spectators were really only at the block where the television cameras were. Of course we totally rocked in a hypothermic sort of way.

For our effort we got to attend the game. Where it started to snow. But, we sat there until the clock showed all zeroes and B.C. collected another "W." Some friendly fans from Boston even gave me a B.C. Eagles ball cap because the souvenir stands were all sold out. Not a great game but still the only bowl game I've ever attended. And, it kept snowing.

Texans are idiots when they get snow. Some would say most other times, too, but I won't say that here. Partly because of the 1 inch of snow that fell and mostly because of the numerous accidents the locals were having trying to drive on the white stuff, our trip was extended an extra night.

Over reaction to moderately crummy weather always reminds me of marching in the Cotton Bowl Parade. Maybe someday I will return to see my team, the Iowa State Cyclones, play in it. Only time will tell.

**"See people rocking
Hear people chanting
Feeling hot hot hot"**
Hot, Hot, Hot – Buster Poindexter

The water heater at our home shot craps recently. As a friend and I wrestled the old carcass out of my basement and eased in the replacement the necessity of a reliable source of hot water was hammered home. I was reminded of my days on the West Harrison basketball team our senior year, a year in which we went totally defeated.

That I was able to be a starter was a huge sign that our team was desperate for warm bodies to take the court - I still can't sink a ten-foot jump shot with any regularity. Nor can I hit a free throw, dribble, d-up, or dunk. Some things just don't change.

We did, however, have our post-game secret weapon.

One of the benefits of having a school gymnasium that was several decades old is that the locker room facilities were lacking in amenities and creature comforts. The "home" and "visitor" locker rooms were side-by-side and barely large enough to hold ten people each.

The home locker room was the one that was the least moldy. Win (yeah, right) or lose, we knew to shower quickly because the secret weapon could backfire. The trick was to flush the toilet while the opposition was showering. The sudden loss of cold-water pressure would cause a surge in the hot water. Not quite scalding but uncomfortably hot.

FLUSH.

Muffled shriek of temperature shock from next door.

FLUSH.

Muffled "Hey, knock it off!"

FLUSH.

Muffled "!@#% $% #$% #$% $% &R^%!"
I doubt that they spoke to their mothers that way. The visitors' showers always ended sooner than they wanted. We may have stunk on the court but the Away teams usually had to stink on the bus ride home.

I hope the West Harrison teams are more skilled than we were because I imagine the showers in the new school don't have the same potential for retribution that our old plumbing had.

The new water heater in my home works just fine, too.

"Oh Say Can You See?"
Star Spangled Banner – Francis Scott Key

The last time I was back home I saw that the water tower had been painted again. Missing was a memento left by my friend, one Don Juan, in the summer of 1986.

Like many summer nights that year, it was late and very warm which was quite conducive to creating a seemingly unquenchable thirst - which we valiantly tried to quench anyway.

Around 11 p.m. I took a ride on Juan's Hondamatic (automatic transmission) motorcycle. About two miles west of Mondamin it occurred to me that I was riding a motorcycle without a license, without a helmet, and with only one hand on the handlebars (beverage bottle in the other) at above the posted speed limit. In a rare exhibition of rational thought, I returned to the Slab and gave the bike back to Juan.

But, we were still bored. I don't recall who thought it would be a good idea, but the suggestion was made that a glass bottle filled with a carbonated beverage would make a really big splash if thrown from the top of the water tower onto the street below. One of the others on the Slab supplied the full bottles that night – we weren't about to use our own. The rest provided copious amounts of encouragement for throwing one off the tower.

Juan scrambled up the ladder first and I followed. Obviously, since I was the one more uncomfortable with heights, I had the beverage bottle and climbed more slowly using just the one hand (go figure). Grab a rung with the free hand, step up, grab with two fingers on the bottle hand <CLINK>, Grab a rung with the free hand, step up, grab with two fingers on the bottle hand <CLINK>, Grab a rung with the free hand, step up, grab with two fingers on the bottle hand <CLINK>. All the way up the tower.

We managed to make it to the catwalk at the base of the elevated tank unscathed. The bottle had not broken though I had banged it against half the ladder rungs during the climb.

My tolerance for excessive elevation was maxed out at the catwalk - it had a guardrail of sorts and seemed as safe as it could be 150 feet above the ground. With a great sense of anticipation, I lobbed the bottle over the railing.

We watched as it quickly gained speed and momentum - it was really going to smack the pavement hard. Then the unlikely occurred. Just when we expected the bottle to explode spectacularly, it hit a power line that "caught" the bottle, stretching and slowing it to a stop - somewhat like a person catching an egg in an egg toss contest at the Harrison County Fair. The taut power line then rebounded and lofted the bottle a few feet up into the air where it then fell the remaining twenty or so feet and shattered on the street, just the same as if someone had unremarkably underhanded an empty into the air from the Slab.

I couldn't have hit that line more perfectly if I tried all night. What a colossal disappointment. I was ready to make the long, slow climb back to the ground but Juan was more adventurous.

While I stood on the relatively safe catwalk, he climbed the ladder up the side of the tank and then continued on up the conical top of the tank and stood up on the peak, straddling the tank's lightning rod, as though he were King of the, well King of Mondamin.

Like Columbus or Hillary, he felt the need to symbolically commemorate his feat. I am so glad he didn't tumble off the tank at this time, but somehow he managed to remove his tidy-whities without falling and knotted them to the lightning rod. With his "flag" in place he stood silently for a moment to take in one last view of the town and then came back down the tank to join me in returning to terra firma.

Needless to say, the group still gathered on the Slab was disappointed with the display. But, for several years if you looked really close at the top of the water tower you could see Juan's flag waving in the breeze.

"Might as Well Go for a Soda"
Go for a Soda – Kim Mitchell

For many of us in high school, the weekend started - and often ended - by meeting at the Slab. Just a 25 feet by 40 feet (now) parking area next to the 100 plus year-old, two story brick building that used to be Iverson's Grocery Store.

Hard to imagine Mondamin having a grocery store but when Iverson's was open it was the second store in town, along with Keith's. Of course, when both stores still existed there was also Billy's Bar & Grill AND The Office eating and drinking establishments in addition to the cafe located in what eventually became Yuck, Muck, and Duck's Bicycle shop. All gone now.

But, the slab remains. Most of the memories I have of those nights wasted on the slab (yeah, that one reads a couple of different ways) involve one of our older friends visiting Billy's across the street every few hours for us to get a case of the Beast (the "Beast" wasn't just my truck, it was also one of Milwaukee's cheapest, er, Best, products).

The funniest thing I remember happening at the Slab, though, didn't involve the Class of '86. It did, however, start a small feud amongst a couple of the Class of '84 members. A small group of us were on the Slab late one Friday night, trying to throw empty aluminum cans up onto the roof of the Iverson building - which is not as easy as one would think.

The Slab was about half the size it used to be because a two bay carwash had just been built on the west side of the Slab. Surprisingly popular, apparently successful, and, best of all, it created a small area between it and the brick building that was secluded enough to become the accepted area at which you could go see a man about a horse.

To augment the carwash income, the owners installed in front of the divider between the two bays, what I believe was the first outdoor pop machine in Mondamin. Great for the hours that neither store was open if one desired a chilled 12 ounce can of Pepsi, Pepsi, Pepsi, or 7-Up, for, say, a mixer. Oh, but the life of a pop machine can be wrought with danger. As we bounced empties off the side of Iverson's building, none of us knew the peril that faced that poor Pepsi machine.

What, with its dual exhaust bellowing, we heard the Ford F-150 known as Old White when it was still a mile or so east of town. It sounded to be moving at a pretty good clip, too. It didn't slow down much as it got closer to town, and closer to the elevated railroad crossing just cattywaumpus about 100 feet from the Slab.

Most of us have either jumped those tracks or been in a vehicle that jumped the tracks and know that the little bounce after touchdown can lead to an undesirable loss of vehicular control. So, we all moved behind my Blazer, the Beast, so we could see the jump but not get killed by the crash that was likely to follow.

Old White was throttled back, though, just before the tracks so there was no jump. We still got a show, however. The truck went about 200 feet past the Slab, engaged the parking brake, and went into a slide in front of Keith's Store. Then, with a teenager's brashness, the driver stomped on the accelerator and did a donut right then and there in the street.

The 302 cubic inch engine in that truck was surely in the yellow, if not red, as the truck started its second doe-nee. But, those tires must have been a little too new, had a little too much tread, because the second and third donuts got more and more elliptical and the truck crept back towards us on the Slab.

On the forth donut realization that things were not going well finally broke through and he let up on the gas just as the tires regained complete traction and launched the truck straight at the carwash.

I've seen people punched in the stomach before and witnessed how they double over and that is exactly what this poor pop machine did when Old White's bumper rammed into it.

Things got really quiet for about thirteen seconds, then Old White restarted, was jammed into Reverse just long enough to get off the pop machine and back onto the street, then ground into Drive and launched over the tracks and back out of town.

Now, I could have sworn that this whole event spanned several minutes, but it only was about 90 seconds from first donut to hasty retreat. It was only about 20 seconds after the retreat that we, the witnesses, processed a couple of facts: a soda machine is very expensive and the destruction of one is certain to spark some form of physical confrontation.

We all left the Slab early that night and got the hell out of town as a brown, sticky pool of Pepsi slowly formed under the machine while a light gray smoke drifted above the remains of the refrigeration compressor. It was a few weeks before things got worked out between Old White's driver and the carwash management, but that will always be the night that Old White failed the Pepsi Challenge.

"Is there a problem with the earth's gravitational pull?"
Dr. Emmett Brown in the movie *Back to the Future*

Here's one for my technologically oriented friends. Our computer lab, that glorified coat closet next to Split's math classroom, consisted of two black Apple II+'s (built by Bell & Howell under license from Apple) and one beige Apple IIE and one snow beige Apple IIc built by Apple. They were fully loaded: the II+'s had 48 Kilobytes of RAM and 14" color (eight colors, I think) monitors and two each 5 1/4" floppy disc drives. The IIe and IIc were about the same except with 64kb of RAM and had a slightly faster Motorola processor. The real workhorses in that tiny room, though, were the 9 pin dot matrix printers.

There were printers connected to just two of the computers so if you needed a hard copy you had to be in the room early enough to get a printer equipped system. Their paper was on continuous rolls, they used ribbons much like the Selectric typewriters in Chuck's typing class used, and they only laid down type when the printer head was moving from left to right. And, they were loud, especially when all both of them were printing at once. They were relics when we got into high school and Split, our math and science instructor, was just itching to get rid of them.

When we were juniors a few hundred dollars had been budgeted by the school board for Split to buy new printers. Much to my surprise, he showed me a mail order ad in *Byte* magazine for some company called Okidata. "Cheap, quiet printers" was the claim. We had never heard of them as they had only been in existence a short time. Throwing caution to the wind, he jumped in with both feet and ordered two of them.

They turned out to be really good printers; fast, quiet, clear, and fast. And, quiet. Just as advertised. Watching the "logic seeking" print head place ink on the paper while moving in either direction was almost entrancing. His gamble on an unknown company paid off. The company is a little better known now.

The best part, though, was the disposal of the old behemoths that had been replaced. Split lived up to his word. He had always said that he was going to do something dramatic to the relics and drama was what he provided. The day the new printers were brought on line and tested out ok, he took the old printers up to the second floor of the south building (the one built in 1890) and opened a window. He had a huge grin on his face as he took out the window screen. The smile got even larger as he hoisted one of the dingy, yellowed printers over his head and chucked it out with a cathartic heave.

As he was pitching the obsolete refuse out of the school building window, a small group of technophiles (nerds) that had gathered for the event watched and cheered as the outdated technology obeyed the laws of gravity and Newton and crashed to the earth with a satisfying crunch. I had an Annual Staff camera with me and took photos of the whole event, including the wrecked remains of the outdated equipment that littered the lawn. What a great day for science; Galileo would have approved.

"Do you want to play a game? "
WOPR's challenge in the movie *Wargames*

Among the hundreds of papers that I have found from my days in high school were a few dozen pages of computer printouts of ancient computer code. There were also several pages more of handwritten snippets of programming that never made it onto a floppy. It was all vintage BASIC, line numbers delineating the sequential order of progression, written long before WYSIWYG and Visual were notions, and is now nearly incomprehensible.

The most powerful computer at my disposal in high school had only 48 kilobytes of random access memory, compared to the 3 gigabytes of RAM my home computers have now - about a magnitude of 66000 change. To cram the farm finance program I wrote for my dad into 48k RAM, I dispensed with proper programming protocol and used neither remarks nor comments and used multiple commands per line number. But, it worked. Dad said when he took the year end printout to his tax preparer (around 1982 or 83) it was the first time the guy had ever seen someone with a computer generated report instead of a shoebox filled with receipts.

The program I wrote for Dad was a great learning experience about developing software to be used by people who weren't geeks, nerds, or technophiles. I figured out some tricks for trapping user input errors and also a thing or two about preventing the program from being accidentally stopped. Good experience for me since I just knew I was going to be a computer programmer when I grew up.

At the time I programmed in BASIC partly because it was simple but mostly because it was what my TRS-80 Model 3 computer and the Apple II computers at school booted to. Sure, there were other languages available such as COBOL, PASCAL, and FORTRAN but they cost a lot of money to purchase.

One day when I was a sophomore in high school (1983-84) my Mom drug me to the Westroads Shopping Mall in what was then west Omaha but is now central Omaha. While she and my sister shopped I ended up at the Radio Shack in the mall's lower level. Radio Shack was the distributor of the TRS line of computers (Tandy-Radio Shack) so I usually hung out there to see what the next generation of hardware would be. This particular day I was bored and all that was on display was a computer much like the one I had at home. When the lone clerk was off helping someone else I tripped the power button and waited for the prompt to reappear on the monitor. When it appeared I typed in a quick hack of a program, keyed RUN, and then sat down on a bench in a common area near the store entrance that gave me a view of the computer.

The computer looked innocent enough, just sitting there on its stand at the front of the store with the straightforward question "Enter your name?" on the screen, the cursor blinking expectantly.

A family of three found it first: a dad, mom, and child of about the age of 10. It was as much an exercise of psychology as it was of programming. This unfamiliar machine was issuing the man a command and he obliged. Maybe he saw it as a test of computer literacy, requiring only that he correctly type his name and hit the ENTER key. The father passed with flying colors. After he entered the data, the computer responded causing all three people to shriek and quickly walk away.

Next a group of four youngsters, each appearing to be twelve or younger, walked up to the display computer. The program had reset itself and was again awaiting a name.

The first youth approached it and read the message. Using the two-finger hunt-and-peck method, he quickly typed in his name. After reading the computer's reply he began to laugh hysterically. He motioned his friends over to the terminal. Each went through the same drill, each having the same reaction to the response. It was their collective laughter that snared my final victim.

The clerk was intrigued by the humor the demonstrator computer had elicited. Seeing the clerk approach, the group of boys scattered. When the clerk arrived the program again beckoned "Enter your name?" She complied. The screen then displayed the response that both the family and the group of boys had seen:

"Well, [clerk's name], I think you stink and I think your mother stinks, too!"

She immediately hit the BREAK button to stop the program. That did nothing because I had disabled it. When that didn't work she hit the power switch and turned off the computer - and didn't power it back up, ending my fun for the day.

I think the code I used was something like this:

10 CLS : POKE 16396,23 : INPUT "Enter your name" A$: PRINT :
PRINT "Well, ";A$;", I think you stink and your mother stinks, too!" :
FOR X=1 TO 25000 : NEXT : GOTO 10

10 was a line number for this (one line) program. CLS cleared the
screen of all text and graphics. POKE 16396,23 was a command I
learned when writing the finance program that disabled the BREAK
key. INPUT A$ is the command and variable that was used to store
the persons name. PRINT just put a blank line on the screen. The
second PRINT put the words in quotations on the screen and also
inserted the name that was entered. FOR X=1 TO 25000 and NEXT
was a way to make the computer count from 1 to 25000, a crude way
to delay the program from doing the last command until after the insult
had been read. GOTO 10 was the final command telling the
computer to loop back to Line 10 that started the whole process over
(see beginning of this paragraph).

Well, Moore's Law outpaced my abilities and I never became that
computer programmer I thought I would be. The world may be a
better place because of that.

"My Old Man is a Television Repairman, He's Got this Ultimate Set of Tools"

Jeff Spicolli in the movie *Fast Times at Ridgemont High*

I think most people with whom I grew up would agree that every now and then I was not above playing a prank. "Prank," "mischief," "hooliganism," "felony," insert whatever term you wish.

One of the excellent instructors who taught me a great deal also had a habit of really stressing particularly important points at the chalkboard by driving the chalk into the slate for emphasis. He also woke nappers by winging one of those wood and black felt chalkboard erasers at them, but that's already widely known by most West Harrison grads. (Smack - POOF! cloud of chalk dust and a telltale white mark on the shirt to let everyone in school know you dozed off in Physics).

I digress. The chalk in that classroom took a beating daily; the splinters of what just seconds earlier had been full pieces of chalk littered the chalkboard tray. As spectacular as that carnage could be, I thought it could be better.

One evening in 1984 I bought a box of chalk and took it out to Dad's tool shop. In what turned out to be a much slower and frustratingly delicate process than I had envisioned, using a drill press I broke four pieces of chalk. Using that same press I drilled out the centers of four other pieces. The resulting tubes of drilled chalk looked like short, brittle straws.

Having not really given this endeavor much thought, I had no idea how to plug the holes in the ends. I stuffed a wad of paper in one end; that looked bad. I tried a glob of Elmer's Glue; that looked worse. I gave up on finding a quick solution, took a chunk of one of the broken chalk pieces, and started spinning it in sandpaper until it was worn down to a cone. I pushed the cone into one end of the chalk tube and then sanded the end down until it looked just like a normal piece of chalk. Perfect. I sanded down more cones and plugged the ends of the remaining tubes, breaking one in the process.

I carefully wrapped the remaining three pieces in tissue ("Kleenex") and took them into the old building (built in 1890) the next morning. I got to Trigonometry class early and put the three pieces of doctored chalk in the tray. This was going to be good. It didn't take but five minutes into class when the first RAP of emphasis was made on the board. And, the damn chalk didn't break.

111

The next point of importance however resulted in small cloud of dust and a handful of pulverized chalk. Success. It even elicited the trademark chuckle of the instructor. Drill Press: $500. Box of chalk: $0.89. 3 hours of doctoring chalk: Free. Making Splitt bust out his trademark laugh: Priceless.

Addendum: Our instructor left the chalk in the tray so the joke could be replayed on the next instructor. Except, there weren't any more classes in that room that day. However, that night there was an adult education computer class taught by an instructor from the Area 13 education office out of Council Bluffs. I have it from a reliable source that one of my chalks blew up in the instructor's hand that night and, with a very puzzled look on his face as he stared at the tubular remains, he was heard to say, "Why in the world would anyone buy hollow chalk?"

"We Thank You for Your Support"
Bartles & Jaymes

The first time I ever heard the word "clique" was when I had the extreme misfortune of watching an episode of Square Pegs when I was freshman in high school. Mods, preps, valley girls: all the rage on the TV but nothing like the kids I knew in school.

I asked my uncle (West Harrison Class of 1978) what cliques our school had and he didn't even have to think about it. "Goons, Jocks, and Nerds." Goons drove the pick-ups and wore cowboy or seed company hats, jocks wore tennis shoes and played in all the sports, and nerds, well, nerds were nerds.

The thing about small, rural schools is the cliques weren't rigidly defined. You couldn't have a football team unless a few goons (a.k.a. goat ropers) took the field. The chorus wouldn't have four-part harmony unless a few jocks lent their pipes. And, nerds, well, nerds were nerds.

I joke about nerds 'cause first and foremost, I was a nerd at heart. I liked geometry proofs, programming in Apple BASIC, playing classical music, wearing glasses. Maybe not wearing glasses, but I did have two perfect attendance certificates.

But, really, when you go to a high school of less than 150, the school itself is the clique.

I was attending a mandatory fun function for work a while ago (got to wear my suit and tie, oh, my) and a conversation there reminded me of a few extracurricular activities from my days back home that frequently mixed the cliques.

First of all, just in case anyone gives a rip, I still dislike formal events; you can put a fresh coat of paint on an outhouse and it will still be full of crap, you can put a suit coat on Jeff and he'll still be full of...well, you get the analogy.

Anyway, a couple of my coworkers and I got to reminiscing about social mixers during high school. You know, the ones like we usually held at Bobby's house - when the parents were away the ceiling fan blade breaks away, right, Robert? It was always worth the drive to the outskirts of Pisgah. Cars and trucks parked in the driveway, on lawn, on the road, and, usually at least one in the ditch. To this day I don't have any idea how or why I ended up driving Tony V.'s silver '84 Chrysler Laser at that last one, but I swear I wasn't the one who broke the window crank (Stoopid things turned the wrong direction). A party indoors, though, that was rare and didn't really capture the ambiance and character of...

...the Remington boat docks out west of Mondamin, past the overpass and beyond the old Burcham place. A full moon, the brown water of the Missouri bubbling by, a fist-fight over whether Bocephus or Bon Jovi was better, and a 16 gallon aluminum cylinder of Milwaukee's cheapest. As the commercial used to claim: "It doesn't get any better than this." This is the same boat ramp that one snowy, winter day a county maintainer got stuck in the river. The operator had been clearing the secondary roads and snow pack built up on the v-blade on the front of his 'grader; his idea to remove it was to nose the blade into the river and have the snow washed away. The road crew guys laughed hysterically when he called over the radio that his rig was stuck in the river and he needed to be pulled out.

For me the key to attending these parties was knowing when to leave. There was bound to be something broken, a fight was going to happen, somebody was going to hurl and/or pass out, and someone was going to put a vehicle into a ditch and maybe on into a cornfield; it was best to not be around for any of those events lest you become an unwilling participant. For example, there was a birthday party at a farm near the Remington boat ramp where I missed the exit time sweet spot by about 30 minutes. It started with Birthday Boy and Best Friend arguing and ended with Best Friend driving over Birthday Boy's foot with a four-wheel drive pickup. Or, it might have been the other way around; I was too busy trying to not get run over by said truck as it sped away from the smooshed foot.

There is a small park south of Little Sioux that was a popular gathering spot. The last time I stopped to visit, the revelers were starting a bon fire to keep themselves warm. Wood was scarce and a split rail fence disappeared shortly after I departed. No one froze that night.

There is still a battle scar in my own home that 1) nobody ever did during 2) a gathering that never occurred that 3) probably involved a portable television being moved from one room to another by 4) someone who was never at my house. A pretty good gash was put into the drywall but the next day a classmate came over, played the part of Bob Villa, and gave a demonstration on the proper application of Spackle. That's the only incident I will ever, ever, ever remember happening at my house and I suggest that no one else remember anything more, too.

Out west of Modale, towards the sand pits near Tyson's Bend were any number of timbers and farm fields that are perfect for a large group of people to congregate. As I mentioned another time, the drawback to being in a field with only one entrance is that there's a bottleneck when people need to leave quickly when, say, I arrive with a red rotating light on the top of my truck like I did out by Dugdale's place near the Powell house, or when real police officers join the party as they were sometimes wont to do.

Some people liked the spillways up north of Little Sioux, others liked the unmaintained road to Sawmill Hollow, but after Lonnie's accident I stayed away from parties near water. The abandoned missile base south of Missouri Valley was another place I never visited, partly because I didn't want to have the Beast breakdown somewhere very inconvenient, mostly because no one asked.

The Slab was always (and will always be) my favorite spot to gather. On any given weekend it was not unusual to find nerds, jocks, and goons gathered on the Slab (nothing says truce like a lukewarm Milwaukee's Best). Maybe Dave's classic Nova or Todd's Trans Am or Brad's Mach 1 Mustang, or even Al's Impala sedan would be there, trunk open so the 6x9s and 100 watt amp could play Z-92 loud enough to hear over the occasional Union Pacific coal train. Not a necessarily a good idea, just a good time.

Somehow, someone was usually able to come up with a keg or a few cases of something, perhaps a premium beer like real Budweiser, but more often a lesser brew like Milwaukee's Best - well, dammit, if you don't like it put more money in the hat when it's passed around.

While that was good enough for most of the guys, you still needed something a little sweeter if you wanted a more gender diverse crowd. Everyone remember what hit the market about that time? Nothing says "party" like Frank and Ed, the two goofy looking old dudes on the cardboard cutout next to the four-packs of Bartles & Jaymes wine coolers. Green bottles, one flavor, about 11 proof - what a great invention.

I thought it was best when you went to McDonalds (had to drive to Council Bluffs or Omaha to find one) and ordered a float without the pop - yes, I mean just ice cream in a cup - and then poured a B & J over it to make a wine cooler float.

Sure, it was a little like putting sugar on Lucky Charms, ultra-sweet yet magically delicious. Fortunately, Sun Country leapt into the market with a wide variety of flavors and, more importantly, introduced the wine cooler two liter bottle. Volume, volume, volume.

Nothing like developing bad habits early that take decades to break. My recommendation today would be to head over to the Cedar Brewery in Cedar Rapids and order one of their Root Beers for a float. Brewed in-house, darned tasty, and a lot less likely to make you drive through Neil's cornfield when you miss that sharp turn on Iowa 75 next to the interstate overpass.

"The Hills Fill My Heart with the Sound of Music"
The Sound of Music - Oscar Hammerstein II

I went to our nephew's high school choral concert in Cedar Rapids recently. Although it was a swing choir with mostly contemporary music and a lot of choreography, it still made me think of my chorus and band days back at good old West Harrison.

Our practices – and concerts – were held in the gymnasium. Practices began with setting up four rows of thirteen to eighteen folding chairs on the basketball court in the gymnasium for the band on Mondays, Wednesdays, and every other Friday, or pulling out the student section of bleachers on the stage/basketball court sidelines on Tuesdays, Thursdays, and the other Fridays for the chorus.

I understand they are designing a new performing arts addition to the new school building but I have no earthly idea how they will reproduce the acoustical qualities of the old gym. I know my tenor saxophone resonated much more nicely off the free-throw line and glass backboard at the high school in Mondamin than it did off the hardwood court and tin backboard at the elementary/junior high school gym in Modale.

But, really, who can forget those great music stands we used? The music holder was made from a heavy gage stamped steel, the post a thick walled steel pipe, and the whole works kept upright by an industrial duty cast iron tripod base. All nicely covered in a utilitarian black crinkle paint finish.

If you got to practice a little late you would likely have to take one of the crummy stands with all of its bolts loosened to the point where the music holder would fold up with no warning and dump all your sheet music onto the floor or have a stripped nut on the cast iron base so that the stand would oscillate your sheet music in big, lazy circles, sorta like the spinning plates on long sticks those vaudeville filler acts used to do. I believe the stands were bought second hand from the pit orchestras after Vaudeville exhaled its final breath.

However, I think we all know that the best part of band practice was the marksmanship drills that several of us in the trombone, trumpet, and saxophone section held during lulls. Those old steel folding chairs (some having "Little Sioux High School" stenciled onto the chair back) we used for both practice and, sadly, concerts, which are more commonly used to smite professional wrestlers during single fall bouts, had hard rubber feet on the chair legs. Those came off quite easily. The more unsophisticated miscreant might take off one of those and throw it at someone. Taking one of those off the ol' melon might sting a bit, or, more cliché-ally, even put an eye out. But, we could throw an object at someone any time of the school day.

It was only during first period of Mondays and Wednesdays (and every other Friday, natch) however, that we could slip one of those oh-too-convenient projectiles from the leg of our chair and, when Bruce the Director was chewing out a trumpet for missing a mark, whip it at not a Freshman, not at the much too accessible basketball hoop, but at more difficult and more bandly targets, the tubas played by Mac and Lewey.

Sure, maybe if we had put that much effort into our basketball games we wouldn't have gotten our asses handed to us on such a regular basis. A ball through the hoop only gave us two fewer points in the margin of defeat stats but a well thrown rubber foot from a steel folding chair would hit the bell of a tuba with a very satisfying "clang" followed by a series of metallic rattles as it fell deep into the brass bowels of the bass instrument. I also remember hearing a considerable amount of swearing but that was usually covered by others cheering the beauty of the well-placed shot.

Over the 'bone section, off the bell of the bassoon, "CLANK!" Nothing but brass. Still music to my ears. Kinda makes one wonder how we got all those 1's at the music contests...

"Janet, Janet bo Banet Bonana fanna fo Fanet"
The Name Game – Shirley Ellis

For several years I have had a real weakness with people's names. I remember John-O was a good friend in Kindergarten. I had "difficulties" with a girl named Shaleen in First Grade. I know Cindy went to school with us in Modale in Second Grade. Angie joined us in Third Grade. Deidra was in our Fourth Grade class. John was in our Fifth Grade class – he took me fishing at Ten Mile Lake in Minnesota one summer. Those are just a few names of kids that only spent a year or two in our school before moving away that leap into my mind when thinking of West Harrison – Modale campus.

But, now when I meet someone, regardless of how many times I silently repeat the name to myself or how many mnemonic devices I employ, the name is instantly gone. I thought it was just a result of becoming middle-aged but the roots actually extend much further back.

One afternoon when we were juniors in high school I made the mistake of being in the high school gymnasium when Mr. Smith was doing a sound check on the public address system. There was going to be a wrestling meet that evening, the last home dual of the season, so it was Parents Night. Though I had never done it before, Mr. Smith chose that night to have me do the announcing for the meet.

Since it was Parents Night I would be introducing not only the wrestlers but also their parents. Mr. Smith handed me the team roster for the meet and told me to announce the parent names and ask them to stand after I gave each wrestler's name.

No problem. I had known most of these guys for over a decade; I could do it in my sleep. So, I winged it. 103, 112, 119, 125, 130, 135, 140, 145, 152, 160, 171, 189, 215, 275; if we had a competitor for the weight class, I belted out his name and the name of his parents and had them stand up.

There was a murmur, though, that ran through the crowd when I gave out Brian's name but I didn't pay any attention to it. I learned later it was because I announced the wrong names for his parents: got his step-dad's name correct but said the name of his step-dad's ex-wife instead of Bri's mom. Crap. I couldn't apologize enough for my stupidity but once you hose things up over a public address system, your error is forever public.

My war with names began in 1985 and I have been losing it ever since.

"But a mob without any man at the head of it, is beneath pitifulness."
Huckleberry Finn by Mark Twain

While in high school I personally saw REO Speedwagon, Loverboy, Pat Benatar (to see the opening act Red Ryder), Styx, and Def Leppard at Omaha's Civic Auditorium, and Stevie Ray Vaughn at the adjoining Music Hall. I have driven by the new Qwest Center and it looks to be a much nicer place than where I saw most of those bands.

General Admission seating was so bogus; I remember arriving with my friends several hours early so we could be the ones at the front of the line shoved up against the metal gates, waiting for the professional event staff (thugs in tattered t-shirts that said "Staff") to open the doors. We would then sprint through the building to the "best" seats: first row of the first balcony closest to the stage (floor access cost extra). It's no wonder those kids died at the Who concert in Cincinnati in 1979 with the total lack of control of GA seating provided.

As I recall, REO Speedwagon's set was almost exactly like their Double Live tape (yeah, cassettes back then), Loverboy was very entertaining (they had lasers, an expensive novelty at that time) for a pop band, Def Leppard was good even though most people only knew two of their songs (*Pyromania* and *Rock Rock 'til You Drop*) and I could feel the heat from their stage show's pyrotechnic explosions. Though I went to see her opening act, Red Ryder, Pat Benatar actually put on a pretty good show, too.

Although I was 35 years old the first time I went to Las Vegas, I'm pretty sure I can say that the Styx concert I saw in 1986 was the first Vegas style show I had seen; very much choreographed and lots of production with the video screen and light show - way too commercial though their early music still sounded good.

By far the best show I saw was the Stevie Ray Vaughn concert that my best friend, Mac, talked me into seeing. It was at the Music Hall instead of the Civic and had reserved seating. The opening act was the Gregg Allman Band (what was left of the Allman Brothers) and was really pretty good. But, to see who was, at that time, the best living guitar player was indescribable.

Unlike the concerts in the Civic Auditorium which tended to be so loud your ears would ring for three days, the Music Hall was more reasonable and the acoustics were much better. No fancy lighting, no explosions, no lasers, just a guy, his guitar, and his excellent backup band, Double Trouble. It was as close to seeing Jimi Hendrix as I will ever get.

I had an opportunity two years later to see him again in Omaha but decided to wait until he came to Ames. He was killed in a helicopter accident a couple months later. Seeing SRV was the highlight of my concert-going days.

"We come from the land of the ice and snow"
Immigrant Song – Led Zeppelin

While channel surfing one chilly evening I had the misfortune of bumbling onto the Winter X Games on ESPN. Normally, I only give each channel five seconds, tops, (its part of the Guys Code) but between seconds three and four at the Entertainment and SPorts Network, I paused. Had to, really, as I was unable to divert my eyes from the spectacle on the screen.

I thought I had found a rerun of a horror movie but I was mistaken. Some dude with a 1 by 12 strapped to his feet had just attempted a "frontside 1080 into a cab 1080" on some snow covered silage pit the announcers called a "Super Pipe."

Unless all that jargon is new slang for "the agony of defeat" I still don't know what it means. Dude went grill first down most of that snowy hillside; that should've knocked him (more) senseless but he hopped right up and ambled over to the camera fronted by a Gen Why announcer-babe.

I was about to pull the trigger on zapping on to ESPN2 (the Deuce) when the snowboarding klutz pulled off his helmet and balaclava to reveal a face profusely perforated with piercings. What the hell? It looked like he had done a face-plant into a tackle box and bore a slight resemblance to Pinhead of *Hellraiser* movie fame.

Anyhoo, as the "athlete" stammered through a nearly unintelligible string of "dudes" and "ya knows" I returned to channel surfing dreading the future that awaits we Gen X/Gen Y 'tweeners. What depressed me even more is that as unmotivated and chemically dependent these 'Gamers appeared to be, I know from observing the youngsters queuing up at the demonstrator video game consoles in the stores that there's an even greater number of "competitors" out there that never even step foot on a real half-pipe - they just "compete" virtually on Wii's, PlayStations, and X-Boxes.

Who's the bigger slacker: a tatted up pincushion professional snowboarder or a pasty skinned obese couch potato *pretending* to be a tatted up pincushion professional snowboarder? That is the question that reminded me of the national craze that struck when we were high school juniors: *Puttin' on the Hits*.

Years before Ashley Simpson was paid to not sing on *Saturday Night Live*, the less than masculine Allen Fawcett was giving out cash and prizes to people who were good at pretending to sing their favorite

123

songs. No real talent really needed other than having the uncanny knack to be good at feigning musical ability.

And, we of the rural heartland were not immune to this asinine fad. A local action group, Parents Working Against Substance Abuse (or whatever they were called), held their own version of the *Puttin' on the Hits*. Usually, I - and most of the people I knew - would have sat back and ridiculed the others who signed up to compete in such an obviously lame event. But, top prize was a hundred bucks and, well, a hundred bucks is a hundred bucks.

Besides, my best friend, Mac, had an idea. Most of the drivel that was usually "performed" was the new crappy pop 'n' roll that polluted the airways. Mac suggested that we form a group and buck the trend by doing a classic heavy metal song instead. It was just crazy enough to work.

It was around track season time so our group was made up of half of the 2-mile relay team, Al and Nut, with Mac, and me making up the other half. The song Mac chose was the rock and roll classic *Whole Lotta Love*, the only Top Ten hit by the heavy metal pioneers Led Zeppelin. Not the typical POTH fare. It was long, it was short on lyrics, and it had a guitar solo in the middle that lasted several minutes. Perfect for participating yet not really conforming.

To prepare for the show we each read the rock-ography *Hammer of the Gods* (Cable television channel VH1 hadn't yet conceived its *Behind the Music* series) and rounded up props. Nut had it easy: as Robert Plant all he had to do was dress like a British hippie and prance around the stage screaming (pretend) into an old chrome microphone I scavenged from my attic. We got an old drum set for Al to use in his role of John Bonham and painted the ZOSO symbol on the front of it to increase the air of authenticity. I drug out Dad's old Beatle boots and Fender Jaguar guitar; the boots were for me to wear as John Paul Jones - I would use Mac's bass guitar, too - and Mac would use Dad's Fender as Jimmy Page. We would be Zeppelin. We would be the Gods. Pretend ones, anyway.

To ensure a victory we practiced a few times. Al wasn't really a drummer but was to impersonate the greatest drummer to ever die in a puddle of his own vomit, Nut never really listened to 70's metal so had to learn the words and how to preen and strut like a angel dust addict, and I needed to figure out how to look like a bass player. Mac played guitar for real so his role would be easy for him. Or, so it seemed.

Whole Lotta Love has a long, psychedelic instrumental solo in the middle. The real Jimmy Page is famous for playing the electric guitar using a violin bow so we found Mac a bow to use in our performance. After five or six practice sessions we felt we could be as convincing as needed; our ultimate goal would be to make it onto the actual TV game show so one of us could slug that weenie Allen Fawcett.

First things first, though, we had to do the PWASA show at the Mondamin gymnasium. There were actually several "acts" lined up for the competition that night - a Saturday night to keep us off the roads and sober. I specifically remember Al's little brother doing a great Chuck Berry *Johnny B Good*, Philip from the Class of '85 and Stacy from the Class of '88 doing a hilarious *Ebony and Ivory* (I've found that many people still remember that one in particular), my sis doing a fairly convincing Rod Stewart, and Penny and the twins from the Class of '87 doing *Time Warp* from *The Rocky Horror Picture Show* (which made me want to step to the left).

Al gulped down his pre-performance pint of chocolate milk and then we were on. I have to admit it was a lot better than I expected it to be. Nut was always a ham anyway (for track meets he often wore underwear that had "Rub 3 Times and Make a Wish" stenciled on the front) and really put on a good Robert Plant impression. Al pounded away at those drums (pillows stuffed inside them so they didn't make noise) and looked fairly convincing. John Paul Jones was the group introvert so I basically just stood in one place and faked the bass line. But, Mac stole the show.

Don Juan was our pretend Roadie and, just before the guitar solo, ran onto the stage and set out a folding chair and the violin bow for Mac. Mac sat down, pulled out the bow, and made that solo look every bit as x-rated as it is intended to be. At the close of the solo he leapt up and kicked over the chair as Al hit the downbeat perfectly to bring us into the ending of the song.

It was then that pretend groupies we bribed to attend the show charged the stage screaming. For not playing a single note, it felt pretty awesome. As we finished the set we tossed towels to our groupies and stormed off the stage to a pretty good round of applause. By far the best act of the night. There were a few more groups that followed us and then it was time for the judges' decision. We reassembled in the gym to wait to collect our $100.

Later that summer we did a reunion show at a competition in Omaha but suffered from age discrimination: we were beat out by some middle-aged folks "singin" a Mamas and Papas medley. Gag me with a spoon! To this day the song *Monday, Monday* still pisses me off whenever I hear it. After that defeat we abandoned our hopes of making it to the real show and popping that dill-hole announcer in the noggin.

Our faux Zeppelin disbanded after Omaha. The following year we tried catching lightning in a bottle again by reforming as the Who and singing *The Summertime Blues* at another PWASA-esque sponsored contest in the Little Sioux gymnasium. But, apparently the judges felt the need to reward a group of little kids who were only marginally entertaining rather than award first place to the best act comprised of us high schoolers. We got the second place prize of $25. Better than nothing but we still felt shafted. We collected our winnings and went to the Slab to exact our revenge.

$25 turned into four dollars and a bit of change each and a twelve pack of Milwaukee's cheapest offering. Thank you very little PWASA. The magic just wasn't there that night. And, just like that, the amateur lip-synching craze vaporized and was replaced by karaoke. Bummer.

"She thinks my tractor's sexy"
She Thinks My Tractor's Sexy – Kenny Chesney

I made it back home for Thanksgiving in 2007, despite the multitude of morons traveling on Interstate Highway 29 the night before. Really, people, when there is an accident on every freakin' overpass between the municipality of Mound City and hamlet of Hamburg, get a flippin' clue and slow the hell down BEFORE a bridge and maybe you won't end up like the other dipsticks wrapped around the guardrails. Sheesh, I love it when a four-hour drive turns into a six-hour odyssey. Speed kills, people, speed kills. That probably seems a bit odd coming from me; it felt odd typing it.

So, in addition to eating too much and spending quality time with the family (including losing Cribbage to my little brother and Bruce which just ain't right) I got reconnected to my farming roots.

Ha, ha ha, ha ha...the beauty of writing is no one sees when I can't keep a straight face when I type such B.S.

My Dad had been back home for a few weeks helping out with the harvest. The Friday after Thanksgiving, Little Brother and I did a few rounds with Dad in a computer controlled, GPS guided techno wonder Case AFX8010 axial flow combine. I swear the damn thing had the same glass cockpit the new Boeing 787 has. But, the first thing I noticed was it had FM radio – CD player, too. That's probably one of the reasons why I'm not a farmer.

Just one reason.

Dad has officially been out of agribusiness for nearly 25 years but he still feels drawn to farming. He really loves making things grow, be it 100 acres of soybeans or an acre and a half of blue grass. I don't get it; never have, and I have a splotchy yard of bermuda, rye, and crab grasses to prove it. And, he's always known that I don't get it. When I was 11 years old (right around the time of Carter's grain embargo and stagflation) Dad told me if I ever said I wanted to go into farming he would hit me over the head with a baseball bat. Good enough for me.

I lack the focus and concentration the job requires. Like the time I was cultivating the north 80 acres between Kelly Lane and Highway 183. Not something I did often but there I was, guiding the International Harvester 6588 diagonally across the field, tilling what had been a bean field. Ok, I don't know for certain it was an IH 6588; it could have been a 4386, 5088, or even a 3788. Hell, it was red like all the other equipment Dad and my Uncle Duane had. And it only had AM radio.

Anyhoo, cross the field, raise the cultivator, turn, lower the cultivator, cross the field, raise the cultivator, turn, lower the cultivator, what will I do this weekend, cross the field, raise the cultivator, turn, lower the cultivator, ask her out maybe, cross the field, raise the cultivator, turn, lower the cultivator, she'll just say no, cross the field, raise the cultivator, turn, lower the cultivator, why the hell won't she go out with me, cross the field, raise the cultivator, turn, go to the slab instead, lower the cultivator, maybe she'll drive by, cross the field, raise the cultivator, maybe she'll even stop, turn, lower the cultivator, cross the field, nah - probably not, hey, what the hell...

And, just like that, the same section of the field has been crossed four times and a thirty-two foot section of barbed wire fence is stuck in one of the outer shovels of the cultivator. When my mind wanders so does the tractor. I was never asked to do anything more complicated than that. But, I think I would fare better with this newer, self-guided heavy equipment. I don't intend to find out, though. Don't want Dad to crack me over the noggin with that baseball bat.

**"If you're gonna play the game, boy,
ya gotta learn to play it right"**
The Gambler – Kenny Rogers

It seems these days I can't scan through all 74 channels of my basic cable without finding at least six stations airing poker games. Bravo, ESPN, Travel Channel, Fox Sports, TBS, the traditional networks; seems like there needn't be any relevance to the stations primary focus as long as they can find a dealer and a group of characters to bet, bluff, and bicker.

So, card playing is now a national craze and everyone hopes the River will complete a straight or a flush. Big whoop. Cards were a part of growing up back home but the games relied less on chance and more on memory and strategy.

A family tradition was playing Cribbage at every holiday gathering. We were taught the game as soon as we were old enough to be able to count to 31 quickly. Grandpa would play a couple of practice games with the kids before moving up to the real games with my uncles. It was a real privilege to be asked to join the grownups' game. I still get a thrill when beating Uncle Bruce, partly because he has played the game so much on a computer he knows virtually every possible hand in the game, but mostly because he's my great Great Uncle Bruce.

However, most people I knew played Pinochle, Euchre, or Pitch. I played all three, liked Euchre the best, didn't really get into Pinochle, and played Pitch the most.

Like Cribbage, I learned how to play 5 Point Pitch from Grandpa Maule. The rules of the game aren't overly complicated: deal out six cards, go around the table bidding on how many of the points you can make, high bidder leads out the first card which determines the trump suit of that hand, all the cards in the hand are played in 6 rounds (tricks), high card wins the trick unless a card of the trump suit is played then highest trump wins the trick, after all six tricks are played out points are awarded for high trump card of the hand, jack of trump (awarded to whomever captured it in a trick), single joker (awarded to whomever captured it in a trick), low card of trump suit (awarded to whomever played it), and game (determined by whomever captures the most face cards and 10's). The first person (or team) to get 21 points wins the game. Oh, and if a bidder fails to make his bid (goes "set") s/he loses the number of points of her/his bid. To spice up the game, there was also a "shoot the moon" bid where you were guaranteeing to make all five points, which, if successful, meant you scored 21 points and won the game. The advantage of being the high bidder is being able to name trump, making it easier to take points; the fun of not being the high bidder is to take points and set the bidder.

Like the current television shows, though, playing for points isn't quite satisfying enough; real players played for cold hard cash. Much like being asked to play Cribbage with the adults at Thanksgiving or Christmas, it was an honor to be invited to play in a Pitch game for money. The stakes were high: typically twenty-five cents to get into the game and a ten cent fine for going set, though some hard-cores would play dollar games with quarter sets. The money, though, was secondary to the reputation. More important than winning the pot of anywhere from $1 to as much as $2 was becoming known as a good player, someone who not only knew the rules of the game but also knew how to count the cards and knew the tells and tendencies of the other players.

I played at home with family, at my neighbor's house, at the Iverson home in Mondamin, the Gochenour's by Magnolia, at the Office Bar and Grill in Mondamin (high stakes dollar games there), as well as other card parties around Harrison County, but the greatest place with the best players was at little white wooden shack of a country store just down the road from my house.

A wonderful woman named Pearl ran a small gas station/store/produce stand walking distance from home. She had a table, chairs, and a soda cooler that was always stocked with 10 ounce bottles of pop, (including my favorite, Strawberry NeHi) which went for a quarter. A quarter, which coincidentally, was also the price of admission into a game of Pitch at Pearl's table.

Some of the greatest card players I've ever known let me into quite a few games at the table in Pearl's store. There was always a deck of cards on the table (dusted in a bag of cornstarch to keep the old cards from sticking together). She also had a small ceramic container on the table that looked like a large, white porcelain thimble which was just big enough to hold the quarters (and all the dimes from the sets) of the card players: the kitty.

The games were played mostly on rainy days and during the winter (there was farming to be done most of the other time). You could play with just three but most games were with four or more and usually played as partners in the four and six person games. Partners was the best and how you earned a reputation; you wanted to be a person that others wanted in the game. I could hold my own and usually did well enough to pay for my NeHi and a Hershey's bar. What I appreciate more now are the memories.

Pearl, the sweet lady who rarely got too upset with anything was a ruthless player and would work as hard as anyone to set someone, grinning the whole while.

Mervin Earlywine, a great player who always overbid his hand, lead a deuce, and never went set because he professed "your partner's good for one point."

Raymond Iverson, the only man I've ever seen lead a Joker on the first trick and name the trump suit - and still take the trick.

My Grandpa Maule who could remember every card played and had a quip for every trick, as good a partner you could ever have.

My friend, Matt, the Jeff Gordon of Pitch, brash and skilled enough to make his boasts come true.

Mary Jo, one of the harshest and outspoken critics at all our high school sporting events but one of the most clever sharps to sit at the table.

Pat Patterson, a large, bald, imposing figure, would set a person in a heartbeat and never stop smiling.

There were a few others who would drop in and play a hand or two but these were the "regulars" I remember. Nothing would make a miserable afternoon pass faster than any four or six (one time we even had eight) of us sitting around that lopsided table, the kitty filled quarters - and a few dimes, cards being tossed onto the old vinyl table cloth (white with some small flowers, I think), and a scrap of paper with the scores dutifully recorded. The hours passed twenty-one points at a time.

"Wolverines!"
Battle cry in the movie *Red Dawn*

I think it was in 1976 or 1977 that the Rialto movie theater in Missouri Valley closed. I could be wrong but the last movie I saw there was *Midway* and that came out in 1976.

Regardless, until Blair opened its two small screens in the 80's, seeing a movie meant going to Omaha. Even after the Blair Twin opened, it was sometimes a few weeks slow on getting the new releases and the selection was limited to, well, two movies. So, when the closest choices were limited to, say, *Harry and Son* and *Starman* and you wanted something more along the lines of *Red Dawn* then a drive to Omaha would be required.

The monster screen at the Indian Hills on Dodge was the best place but it didn't always carry the same fare that typically interested my friends and me. Invariably, we ended up at the multiplex connected to the Westroads Mall out on (what used to be) the western-most edge of Omaha.

Which my friends, Mac, Ford, and Juan, and I were up to one summer night. It had been a crappy day. I took a circuitous route from baseball practice in Pisgah and was going home via Little Sioux so I could flirt with the girl at the ice cream stand. Instead of getting a caramel sundae, though, I ended up getting a flat tire. This was not an isolated incident; the tires on my truck, the Beast, had a bazillion miles on them and flats were commonplace. Needless to say, I was extremely proficient at the art of tire changing. So, as I had done several times that summer, I changed the tire, but since I had to pick up the guys I passed on the sundae.

Anyhoo, the four of us went to the Westroads to see a flick. We got there too late to catch the evening show and way too early for the late show but, dammit, we were going to see a movie that night so we went ahead and bought tickets for the late show. This left us an hour and a half to kill. So, we drove to the "new" indoor miniature golf and arcade on the northeast corner of 72nd and Dodge for a round of putt-putt. Well, short story long, we lost track of time and didn't notice until twelve minutes before the start of the movie. We had to NASCAR it the sixty-four blocks between the golf place and the theater but we made it in time to see the movie – and even get popcorn, too (they asked if we wanted butter but said no, that yellow oily shtuff they used would be ok).

The movie was awesome; we knew that if it weren't for the near certainty that we would be wiped out by nuclear devastation when the Strategic Air Command base in nearby Bellevue was destroyed that we would be part of the resistance fighting those commie bastards. At least, that was what we were telling one another as we walked across the parking lot to the Beast.

Which had another flat tire. Crap. Since I was in a hurry to pick up the guys I hadn't gotten the other tire fixed so there was no spare. Fortunately, there was a Firestone shop in the lot next to the mall to which we rolled one of the flats. It was closed but there were still guys inside working. We got their attention and told them the problem we had: two flats, fifty miles from home, no other garage near. They said, "Sorry, closed." We tried appealing to their humanity but they would have none of it.

Being the time before cell phones, we had to search out a pay phone that had both a phone book and a dial tone. We managed to get a hold of Mac's sister who took us and one of the flat tires to a garage next to the Indian Hills theater (go figure). The man at that garage not only repaired the tire in ten minutes but also charged us only two bucks to do it. Mac's sis drove us (and the fixed tire) back to the Westroads parking lot.

With four of us working as a pit crew the tire was changed in just a few minutes, just an hour and a half after the movie ended. With just a little cooperation from those tools inside the Firestone shop we could have been on our way in much less than that.

We thanked Mac's sister heartily as we left. We made sure to drive by the Firestone shop on our way out of the parking lot and made it audibly and visually clear just what we thought of those useless a-holes. Childish? Perhaps. But, we felt better.

"Can I borrow your towel for a sec? My car just hit a water buffalo."
Irwin 'Fletch' Fletcher in the movie *Fletch*

1) Must like football (the real kind, not that soccer fad), 2) must like cold pizza (the food, not the crummy morning show on ESPN), and 3) must like the quote machine movie "Fletch" (the original, not the piece of crap sequel). These are three qualities the perfect woman would possess - according to my friend, Todd. He was joking. I think. Ironically, these happen to be among the many fine qualities his wife possesses (they actually have considerably more in common).

However, I learned an appreciation for football from my wife, never liked leftover pizza unless it was properly nuked, and *Fletch* always reminds me of standardized tests.

It was early in June of 1985. It was a Friday night and we had played a home baseball game in Pisgah against a team I don't recall with a result that is irrelevant. I remember sitting on the hood of my truck, the Beast, parked across the street from Siebel's IGA Grocery Store, and talking to a girl with whom I was infatuated (and a few other people but they don't stand out in my memory like she does) until around 2 a.m. I should have been at home but this girl had not spoken to me like a real person for any amount of time before so far be it from me to bolt early. Funny the stuff you remember after 20 years. Right after she left I told the others "I gotta go, I have to take a test tomorrow."

Such was my preparation for the ACT. Our Guidance Counselor was a pretty cool guy but in some ways I wish he would have stressed a few things a little more, like, say how important that stoopid test could be. I was only 16 - how the hell was I supposed to know half asleep and hung over was no way to go into the test? Actually, it turned out OK but then I've always been pretty good at faking my way through multiple-guess tests. Besides, he did make sure I at least signed up to take the darned thing.

Since there were only a handful of us from West Harrison taking the test we had to go to the Big City to take it at a larger venue. Even though we were students at an Iowa school we took the test at the University of Nebraska - Omaha. I hitched a ride with my pal, Cathy, in her maroon Cordoba (with a bitchin' 360 c.i.d. engine but no Corinthian leather seats), which was nice for my headache. I'm thinking my friends, Mac and Ford, went with us too but I could be wrong. I remember nothing of the drive down or the test itself but oh, the relief when it was done.

It was early afternoon on a Saturday and after making pretty patterns on bubble sheets for several hours we all needed a pick-me-up. Someone said "Movie?" and the rest of us said "sure."

So, most all the West Harrison kids left the exam room and met at the theater. The film that day? *Fletch*. We laughed our collective butts off for two hours. Now, whenever I hear "Moon River, wider than a mile" I think of *Fletch* and the exam - the ACT exam, that is. And, I've never watched that movie all the way through again since.

"The lake, it is said, never gives up her dead"
Wreck of the Edmond Fitzgerald – Gordon Lightfoot

As I drove north for a canoe and camping vacation in Minnesota, I detoured up through Modale and Mondamin to see family before heading on out of the state. As I approached Pisgah I glanced over at the pond just south of town and its still water reflecting the scrubby growth on the shores reminded me of another canoe trip that my friend, T.C., and I once took.

Back when T.C. was a senior and I was a junior in high school, the youngest Knudsen boys and (I think) their friend Troy had a canoe at that pond. They kept it pulled up on shore just inside the brush but we could easily see it when driving to the Pisgah ball field for baseball practices and games.

One afternoon as the team bus was driving along Highway 183 to a game with either Mo. Valley or West Monona I saw the sun glint off the aluminum hull there in the leaves and elbowed T.C. and our teammate, Brian, and told them I had an idea. That night during the post game refreshments on the Slab I told T.C. and Brian to get about twenty feet of clothesline and an empty, plastic milk jug and to meet me at the pond the next day - and, to wear swim trunks.

We all managed to remember this and rendezvoused at the pond that next afternoon. I tied one end of the rope to the bow of the canoe and the other to the handle of the empty 1-gallon milk jug. We then paddled out to the middle of the pond and completed the plan: we tipped the canoe onto its side and allowed it to fill up with water and sink out of site. The jug floated along the surface of the water marking the pond's newest shipwreck.

It never occurred to me at the time how lucky we had been that the owners of the boat weren't there or showed up as we capsized the craft or that the pond was deeper than the 20 feet of rope we had. Better lucky than good.

The next day it wasn't easy to not laugh out loud as the Knuts complained about the @$$ holes who stole their boat. They complained again the day after that. And the next day. And the next day. And the next day. It got a little old after a week.

Every day I always checked the pond for that milk jug, happy to see that it was still seemingly glued to the center of the pond. Surely, someone had to wonder why it didn't move - like those guys who lost their canoe for instance. Finally, a week later as the team bus headed south down 183 past the pond, the laments for the stolen canoe began again. I broke my silence and mentioned that I found it really odd that the milk jug in the middle of the lake hadn't moved in over a week even though it had been really windy several times. Too subtle; the canoe thief-lament restarted.

Finally, T.C. said to shut up already and to be at the pond the next day and he/we would help look for the canoe. We thought they would figure out that the jug was tethered to something, especially when it was pointed out that it had not drifted at all in over a week. But now with no end in sight we were worried that something would happen to the jug and the marker of the missing ship would sink.

We met the loss-ees at the pond the next day and had them swim out to the jug marker with us. We got out to the jug and then just treaded water because we didn't really know what to do next. T.C. dove down to try grab the boat but came up empty. I was about to do the same when Brian grabbed hold of the clothesline and started swimming to shore. The boat slid along the bottom and came to shore with him. T.C. and I swam on in to shore and helped pull the boat out of the water and drain it.

The mysteries of the missing canoe and the immovable floating milk jug had been solved. "We'd have gotten away with it, too, if wasn't for those meddling kids" No, wait, we did get away with it; the victims' whining just got too annoying.

"Creepy, creepy, crawly, crawly"
Boris the Spider – The Who

My friend, T.C., and I decided to go on a hike one night in the summer of 1985. He was dating Jana (now Mrs. T.C.) at the time and had left his car at her house there near the high school. For reasons to this day I still can't reasonably explain we all of the sudden-like got the urge to listen to *Boris the Spider* by the Who on their *Meaty Beaty Big and Bouncy* cassette (cassettes are like a CD only sound worse and last just a couple of months before self destructing into a pile of cellulose spaghetti). Instead of driving my truck, the Beast, from my house back to town - 3.28 miles - we decided we would grab the last of the refreshments and walk it.

So we were walking along Highway 127 just past Spooner's farm when T.C. developed the need to relieve himself. Not wanting to put on a little show (em-PHA-sis on "little") for the passing traffic he crossed the ditch over towards Spooner's pasture. After he emptied out a couple of processed beverages he noticed that there were horses in the pasture. Not being one to pass up a chance to get close to farm animals, he decided he would call them over to pet them.

"Here horsie, horsie, horsie, horsie."

"Here horsie, horsie, horsie, horsie."

He crept through the grass to get closer.

"Here horsie, horsie, horsie, horsie."

He moved a little closer.

"Here horsie, horsie."

They were actually moving closer and he was now to the fence.

"Here horsie, horsie...

...AAAAGGGGHHH!!!!

He had grabbed the fence to climb over to pet the nice horsies.

The *ELECTRIC* fence.

...AAAAGGGGHHH!!!!

I believe it zapped him twice before he could release his grip on the wire. He never did get to pet the horses but we did make it to town. Turned out the cassette wasn't even in his Monte Carlo - it was in the Beast that we had left parked in the driveway back at my house.

"Stop, Snidely Whiplash, in the name of the law!"
Dudley Du-Right in television show *The Bullwinkle Show*

So, one Saturday evening in the summer of 1986, my friend, T.C., and I were leaning up against his white Chevrolet S-10 pick-up that was parked in front of his future wife's house. We had just wasted the better part of a day sitting in a boat on a lake outside of Modale not catching any fish. It was one of those *King of the Hill* moments: just guys standing there, aluminum beverage cans in hand, with the chirps of the crickets and birds interrupted only by the occasional "yep" and/or "uh-huh." The novelty of the conversation disappeared rapidly.

Then, without a word - or, any rational thought - T.C. performed one of those random rebellious acts of stupidity that bored teenagers are often wont to do. He walked over to the street sign that was on the corner of the block. It was a "School Crossing" sign that faced the traffic coming from the east on Highway 183/127 on the north side of the house.

I'd seen others do this before and knew what was going to happen next. He grabbed the creosoted 4x4 post and started shaking it back and forth violently. Because this had been done by several others it took very little time for the post hole to enlarge so much from the shaking that when T.C. grabbed the sign post and lifted, it came right out of the ground. He tossed it down next to the sidewalk, returned to his truck, and retrieved another cold one from the cooler.

"Yep." "Uh-huh."

But, abject vandalism seemed too hollow. I walked over to where the sign now lay on the ground and looked around a bit until I spied the bit of irony I felt the situation needed. Just a few feet from the fallen sign at the highway intersection was a stop sign facing the northbound cross traffic. As T.C. had done a few minutes earlier, I shook the signpost until it lifted easily out of its hole.

But, unlike T.C., instead of just callously tossing it aside, I placed it in the hole left vacant by the school crossing sign, facing the Highway traffic. Then I picked up the fallen crossing sign and placed in the location previously occupied by the stop sign.
As I was completing the switch, T.C. tossed his empty into the back of his pick-up, ran across the highway to the opposite corner, and performed the same switcheroo with those signs. Anyone could (and often did) jerk a sign out of its hole and throw it to the ground and that didn't feel right. Swapping signs around, well, ok, that wasn't right either, but it did seem funny at the time.

To T.C. and me, anyway.

It wasn't until the following Monday when I next saw T.C. and heard who did not see the humor in our redistribution of traffic control devices. Apparently a law abiding out-of-towner and his spouse were driving through Mondamin the morning after the switch was made and came to a full and complete stop at the our freshly re-signed intersection. One of our local law enforcement officers who was born and raised in our community was just coming on duty and was following the out-of-towners. I understand he was swearing profusely after nearly rear ending they who had inexplicably stopped on a State Highway.

The couple was equally shocked that a member of the law enforcement community nearly clobbered them at a controlled intersection. After they proceeded - first visually verifying there was no speeding traffic on the side street - the reason for their unexpected stoppage became apparent to the officer. He was in the midst of a controlled intersection where one had never before existed in his lifetime.

He was still swearing loudly as he ripped the stop signs out of their now ill-fitting holes and tossed them to the ground. The inhabitants of a nearby house, who watched him drive off in a huff, witnessed all this.

Some things to be learned here: 1) Be alert - I recently had an experience similar to that Trooper's only I was at the north end of Modale - who the hell put up those new Stop signs? 2) Traffic Control Devices should only be installed and maintained by trained transportation officials, 3) Unexpected Change is not necessarily good, and 4) I'm not much of a fisherman.

**"So you'd better get out of my way
When I come through your yard
'Cause I've got a bitchin' Camaro"**
Bitchin' Camaro – The Dead Milkmen

To stay with the theme of "poor luck with automobiles," I hearken back to a hot and stiflingly humid summer night in the summer of 1987. My friend, Juan, surprised me with a late evening visit when he pulled into my driveway in another friend's Z-28 Camaro (it had an Air Induction hood; I think it was an '80 model).

We were both quite recently in between significant others and he was looking for someone with whom to drown sorrows. He had found the right man for that job. He came with a case of Bud longnecks. Unfortunately, all but three were already empty which explained the poor parking job he'd done, nearly taking out my seldom-used basketball hoop.

He told me that it was time to take the "Z" back to the owner's place (a house up between Little Sioux and Pisgah) but he was looking for someone to A) help finish the case (ooh, a whole bottle for me) and B) drive the "Z" while he followed in his uncle's car so there would be a way home. Seemed reasonable.

I had never driven a Camaro before so I, being the least impaired (it was a full case of empties just as we turned out of my driveway), took command of the "Z." Wow, even though my truck, the Beast, could top-end around 120 miles per hour, the Camaro had hellish pick-up and cornered a lot better than my Blazer what with its bald tires and worn out ball joints. If only it wasn't so hard to get in and out of the "Z" (bad knees run in the family) I could have loved it.

Anyway, 90 seconds after leaving my house we had covered three miles and were at Juan's place. The plan was he would borrow his uncle's car, drive to the Camaro owner's place, I would follow him, we would leave the "Z" there, and then come back to Mondamin in his uncle's car and maybe look for a fresh twelve to celebrate…well… whatever needed celebrating.

I told him to take it slow and steady because he was still in less than ideal driving condition. He said he would then jumped into the car and rocketed down the highway towards the railroad tracks on the west end of Mondamin. I jumped into the "Z" and launched after him, doing my best to not bottom out on the railroad tracks Juan had most surely jumped on his way out of town.

Just west of Mondamin I turned north on County Road K45 and stood on it; I could see his taillights dimly up ahead of me. The cowl induction flap in the car's hood flipped open and the "Z" went from slow to 100 miles per hour very quickly. Ha, the Beast had a higher top-end. In any case, I caught up with him in just a couple of miles and kept the speeding Juan close - but not too close. He was remarkably in control, all things considered.

Out of habit, we both slowed as we passed Ab's Place bar in River Sioux to see who was there. As I returned my eyes back to the road, Juan had again jackrabbited away from me onto County Road F20 and into Little Sioux.

I was beginning to understand how the Modale Marshall had felt the previous Halloween. I raced through Little Sioux and didn't see him anywhere. I followed F20 all the way to "Z" owner's house and when I got there, no Juan. Major concern since I had not passed him.

I retraced my path back to River Sioux and still no Juan. Once again I drove F20 from River Sioux into Little Sioux, only this time I was only going about 25 miles per hour. I checked all eight of the streets in Little Sioux but didn't see him anywhere. I got back onto F20 and headed north out of town back towards Pisgah - maybe he just skipped the house altogether.

As I got to that big curve just on the north side of Sioux I saw that the gravel in the seal coat that I had just worked on a couple of weeks earlier had two long skid marks that went straight off the road. I broke into a cold sweat and my mouth tasted like I was sucking on pennies (you all know that taste and why).

I pulled onto the shoulder with the "Z"s headlights shining down into the timber that was just off the road. Juan's uncle's car was down there, its hood wrapped around a tree. I felt sick. I knew that Juan was dead and I didn't want to see it.

I drove back into Sioux and found a pay phone. It still had a phone book in it so I called Puggy, the closest classmate I could think of, and told him there had been an accident and I needed help right away and to meet me on the north end of Sioux. I next called Harrison County Sheriff's dispatch and told them I needed to report an accident and I thought it might be fatal.

I went back to the accident scene and waited for Puggy. The Little Sioux volunteer first responders showed up instead. I led them to where the car went off the road and told them what I thought had happened and that I hadn't been down there yet (yeah, I didn't want to be the first to identify the body). An ambulance showed up. A Little Sioux Volunteer Fire Truck showed up. A Harrison County Deputy showed up.

The first responder Emergency Medical Technicians came up from the wreck and said the car was empty. I was struck stupid (ok, more stupid) at that. They pulled me aside and told me they had found a few empties and had thrown them into the trees (after all, who doesn't like Juan?).

A car pulled up behind the fire truck, it was another volunteer fireman. And, he brought Juan with him. They walked up and asked what all the fuss was.

Apparently, since enlisting in the military, Juan had become a chronic user of seat belts, a habit I picked up shortly after that night. The seatbelt, coupled with his 3.2 induced state of relaxation, allowed him to launch his uncle's car off that curve and into that tree without even the slightest scratch. I didn't know if I should be happy or pissed. His uncle was going to be pissed about his totaled car so I opted for happy.

All the emergency personnel returned to their vehicles, shut off their flashers, and headed home. We drove the "Z" back to its owner and he returned us to our homes. I quit shaking by the time I got back to my place.

Puggy, I'm still waiting for you to show up and help.

"You got to get a little mud on the tires"
Mud on the Tires – Brad Paisley

I was looking at a map of Mondamin some time ago (a large scale map yet it still on a 3 1/2 by 5 index card) and saw a street/road that I always recall on rainy days.

North Road: the oil and pea-gravel seal-coat street that turns to dirt just north of town on the west side. No one hardly ever used it because it was rutted so badly, except maybe for parking on a Saturday night or to spray paint "86" on a grain bin.

It was badly rutted, of course, because whenever it rained every fool with a driver's license at the high school would try to see if they could drive their car or truck through the mud from the edge of town all the way over to the highway without getting stuck in the muck.

Usually, this would happen in the morning before school started at 8:30 but after a brief stop at Keith's store for a fresh doughnut and a pop. I knew my truck, the Beast, with its full-time 4-wheel drive and gas guzzling, oil burning, loud as hell, 454 cubic inch engine would have no trouble conquering such easy pickins as a little ol' muddy road so I never joined in the challenge. However, I also knew the Beast could handle it because more than once someone would try to take a two wheel drive truck through this muddy obstacle course and get stuck right around where the road has the sharp 90 degree corner going from north-south to the east-west; right where the grain bin has the "86" spray painted on it.

Anyways, somehow stuck folks would hitch a ride back to school to ask someone with a proper off-roading vehicle, such as myself, to come out to the muddiest portion of North Road to help unstick their vehicle and tow them back to dry, solid terra firma. This is just one of a few reasons why I always had a tow rope in the Beast.

I learned a couple of tricks from my dad about towing that came in handy for these rescue missions. 1) Always use low gear to maximize the towing power, 2) Let the person being towed use their brakes to slow you both, and, most importantly, 3) Just like when giving someone a jumpstart, always, always, ALWAYS let the other driver hook-up to their vehicle.

I vaguely recall pulling the bumper off some dumbass sophomore's car once because they hooked the rope up to the wrong place. THE SOPHOMORE hooked the rope up to the wrong place. So, I knew from experience that the Beast could handle a muddy North Road.

While towing another vehicle. And, I still have that same towrope in my truck today complete with a few bits of North Road mud stuck to it from the last time it was used.

**"If Everybody had an Ocean
Across the USA
Then Everybody'd be Surfin'
Surfin' Like Californ-i-a"**
Surfin' USA – Beach Boys

For some inexplicable reason, I have several stories of stoopid auto tricks. My friends, Ford and Mac, and I were in Mondamin one night after a play practice - had to have been *Diary of Anne Frank* - and we were having a pop on the Slab (a real soda pop, not the barley kind). Bored senseless and on the Slab - not a good combination. I had Z-92 (the Rock) cranking out of the cracked single in-dash speaker of my old Chevy Blazer, the Beast. Even with the Scorpions blaring out *Blackout* in mono while we stood there with Pepsi's in hand, it was boring. Nobody else at all was on the streets in town.

I honestly don't know how the idea arose or who may have suggested it. I would like to think it was because a Beach Boys song was playing on the radio but the Z would never spin oldies surf music. Ever. Anyhoo, somehow I ended up on the roof of the Beast while Mac handled the wheel duties; I stood in wide-stanced low crouch, hangin' ten, car surfin' the mean streets of Mondamin. He said we were only going about 20 miles per hour but I'm pretty sure it was closer to 60. Cowabunga.

On our second lap around the one-mile loop of Mondamin I heard through the "shore" breeze rushing past my ears "Jeff, get off that truck this instant!!" Funny, the ocean wind sounded a lot like my Great Uncle Bruce (yeah, that Bruce, our high school band and chorus director). I looked to my right and about tumbled off the top of my truck. Son of a gun, only one person out and about in the whole freakin' town and he was both a teacher and a relative.

Holy shiitake mushrooms. Mac sped up to flee the raging Bruce, nearly causing me to wipe out. We stopped at the east turnaround of the loop and I got back into the truck. It was enough excitement for one night. We went back to the Slab, all got behind the wheels of our own vehicles, and went home.

Now, I'm sure the fact that we had seen Michael J. Fox do the exact same thing in the movie *Teen Wolf* just a few weeks earlier may have given us the idea. However, I proved on many occasions that I could be stupid of my own initiative, and could have certainly come up with something just as idiotically dangerous without the help of Hollywood - I did on other occasions.

I've also had at least three classmates remind me of what another kind of surfing in the Midwest is like. Apparently, I should know this but I really don't recall it. But, since the witnesses' stories all correlate, it must have happened. What follows is an [slightly edited] account of how the Quonset on (East) Kelly Lane and the grain bin on North Road got their "86" spray-painted on them and how one can surf "Austin Avenue" from River Sioux to Mondamin.

I thought I painted one or both of the "86"s on the grain storage facilities. I was pretty sure I did the one on East Kelly Avenue (the official E-911 street name now) because I saw the other classes painted theirs on there for most of my childhood and had always wanted to see our year up there, too. I was not so sure about the North Road one but that one may have gotten done the same night. Being much older and wiser now - which ain't saying much - I can neither encourage nor condone such brazen acts of stupidity that are about to be described. Anyhoo, here is how another classmate describes some of that evening:

"Yup, you definitely did the one on North Road - in John Deere green. Not only were you crazy to ride on the running boards while [name redacted] was driving, you stood on the open door of the bin which is what, an inch wide? I was "safely" crammed into the front seat on the truck with [names redacted]. Who else was with us? [Name redacted]? Some things are a little cloudy for me, too. I think it started raining. I also seem to remember you having a mug or something that you always drank out of - did I make that up? Weren't we working on our Homecoming float in the Coach's garage that night? I confess, I did the primer brown "86" on Kelly Lane. :) Partners in crime. I won't tell if you won't."

Naturally, I have promised not to tell, either. For the record, 1) The driver of the pickup says 60 mph for the running board surfing - which is something no one should do and I greatly appreciate his ability to keep it between the lines and not tossing me into the ditch or down the highway, 2) Yes, I had a 32oz mug and still have it - it sits on a shelf in my basement as a reminder of all the less than intelligent things I did a long time ago; fun, but stoopid, 3) Yes, we did build a Homecoming float in the Coach's garage out of a hayrack, chicken wire, napkins borrowed from the Missouri Valley Li'l Duffer, and spray-paint. What a fun time.

Given the right conditions, the right group of minds, and a little time, stupid things can - and often do - happen.

"A deer has to be taken with one shot. I try to tell people that but they don't listen."
From *The Deer Hunter*

One Friday night during the summer of either '85 or '86 one of my older, graduated friends, found himself unable to continue driving himself around the county. About 2ish in the morning the decision had been made to leave the Slab in Mondamin and go to the Sunnyside Truck Stop in Missouri Valley to get something to eat. My condition was better than his so I assumed chauffeur duties of his dad's pickup.

The Sunnyside truck stop is located on U.S. Highway 30 at the east edge of Missouri Valley. After a long night of being a complete nuisance to the County of Harrison, there was nothing better than driving to Sunnyside (Open 24 Hours) to get a mediocre cheeseburger, greasy french fries, and a really crummy cup of coffee. But, the service was second to none.

Admittedly, the main reason to go to Sunnyside was because it was the only place open at 4 a.m. But, secondary to its convenient hours of operation was its unparalleled ambiance. Built in the early part of the twentieth century, renovated, well, never, it was a dingy memorial to truck stop history.

Every booth had its own mini jukebox hanging on the wall over the end of the table (10 cents a song, three songs for a quarter). Several booths had telephones though I never sat at one of those. Postcards of the local sites of interest and clear cellophane bags of bulk generic candy hung on chromed wire turning display trees near the cash register, begging to be purchased as you left. The lemon drops were the best in my opinion.

My favorite part of the decor, however, was hanging on the walls. On every bit of open wall space available hung a cat clock. They were available in several different colors and all were accented with rhinestones. The tail wagged to mark the seconds and the eyes would shift back and forth opposite of the tail. There were dozens of these classic beauties hanging around, just waiting and hoping to get the opportunity to go home with one of the many late night patrons to keep time at, presumably, a better place.

So, I had a cheeseburger and several cups of coffee as my friend "dozed off" in the booth. Sunnyside's cheeseburgers were almost as good as the ash-burgers Nettie made at Mondamin's Office Bar and

151

Grill. Almost. Sometime around 3a.m. I finished my late-night snack and helped my friend back to the truck.

My truck, the Beast, was parked on the Slab so we headed back down Highway 127 towards Mondamin. At that time the speed limit was a paltry 50 miles per hour. I always felt that it was my responsibility to prove that the road could be safely traveled at 75 miles per hour (except for the curve at Old Calhoun where it's prudent to throttle back to 65) in hopes that the Authorities Having Jurisdiction would take heed and fix this obvious error - I like to believe my efforts were in some small way responsible for the current 55 mph speed limit. Baby steps, my friends, baby steps.

Anyway, this particular evening was much like many others those years, I was blazing down the highway between the speeds of 50 and 90, there was no moon so I had headlights on (this time), and, as an added bonus, it was someone else's truck and he was unconscious in the passenger half of the bench seat. I had successfully maneuvered through the Old Calhoun curve at a near record speed and was nearing the halfway point between the Valley and Mondamin just south of Melody Oaks, accelerating back up to cruising speed.

For those of you who haven't traveled that road recently (or ever), the Loess Hills are on the east side of the road and to the west is the river bottom farmland. So, anyhoo, I'm at Warp 8 when, all of the sudden, WHAM! THUMP! Thump-thump-thump-thump-thump-thump. The freakin' truck was pulling to the left and trying really hard to toss us off the road and down into a cornfield which, in that area, was a good tumble down a steep ten foot high bank. As I should have expected, a dumbass yearling deer had come ripping across the field, ambled up that bank, and jumped head first into my door, banged into the truck box, rolled under the driver's side rear tire, and blew out the tire with a broken leg bone. Stoopid deer.

The ruckus brought my friend back to life rather dramatically. I managed to drop out of hyperspace and get us stopped on the shoulder. At that point we were close enough to a friend's house near the Melody Oaks subdivision that we were able to walk to his place. More help was needed so another friend, who lived just up the road in the Oaks, was called to come help us change the tire (which I think we may have had to borrow from one of them).

The driver's side box of the pickup was toast (besides caving in the box, there were deer crap streaks down the side from when the deer's body whipped around after jumping into the driver's door. Say it with me: "eeewwww").   My buddy was much more alert now and concerned about the fallout from his dad who had loaned him the truck because his car was in the shop. I was wondering if there would be repercussions for me.

Some dipstick deer kamikazied the truck but I managed to go from 80 to shoulder in just a few seconds without any further loss of life. I was pretty sure the several hundred dollars of damage to the truck would overshadow my semi-impaired driving prowess. After the four of us changed the tire my now wide-awake friend and I managed to get back to Mondamin without further incident but at a slower speed. Much slower. Stoopid deer.

It was a sad day in my existence when I drove down Highway 30 from Logan to Missouri Valley and saw that Sunnyside was no more, falling victim to the same fate as the Tamarac Restaurant: a devastating fire of unknown cause. I now wish I had bought one of those cats - they would probably bring a hefty appraisal on the *Antiques Road Show*.

"I looked in the mirror and a red light was blinkin'"
Hot Rod Lincoln - Charlie Ryan

My birthday falls in what is the second semester of a typical school year. Normally that was inconsequential to my academic existence. Except when we were sophomores in high school. During the 1983-84 school year was when most of the kids in my class turned 16. And, of course, 16 is the most important age a kid can turn (though some might argue 21 is more important but then a 'kid' doesn't turn 21) because that is the last hurdle to driving (legally).

Or, almost the last hurdle as it was for kids like me whose birthday falls in the last half of the school year. Getting a drivers license hinged upon passing Drivers Education and you couldn't pass Drivers Ed until you enrolled in it and (to get to my point) when you were allowed to enroll depended upon when your birthday fell in the calendar year.

First semester was always for the youngest juniors and the oldest sophomores and second semester was for the oldest sophomores and a few of the oldest freshman. For the old Frosh and the old Sophs this timing worked out rather well. For the rest of us it stunk like the 1970's disco craze. Especially for people like me whose birthday fell in the middle of the semester because that meant that even after I turned 16 I still had to wait for another three months of Drivers Ed to complete before I could get my license.

Not that such technicalities mattered a whole lot: like most kids who grew up in the rural part of Iowa, I learned how to drive on a tractor, specifically a Farmall H.

I was in a 90 acre field of corn pulling a trailer loaded with 30 foot sections of 6 inch diameter circle-lock aluminum pipe that my dad and my uncle were unloading. Later the pipes would be joined together to bring water from a well to irrigate the field. Since they were walking along side the trailer dropping off sections of pipe every 30 feet, I idled along in first gear with the throttle was set as low as it would go. Not Iowa Corn Indy 250 type speed but still, I was driving. I was about 10 years old at the time.

Later that summer when the H was being used at a different field I got to drive my uncle's pickup truck to pull the load of irrigation pipe. Nothing against the venerable Farmall, but driving a 3/4 ton Chevy pickup was much more cool, even if was just an automatic going so slow the needle on the speedometer didn't even lift off the peg.

Within a year or two I was driving from field to field taking a pickup to where Dad or my uncle was waiting after moving a tractor or combine. I almost always stayed on the gravel back roads; even the local authorities in a farm community would frown upon a 12 year old driving alone.

I think it was either the summer after our 5th or 6th grade when I first took Mom's Blazer (the truck that a few years later would become the Beast) out for spin without being specifically told to do so. I was playing Cub B baseball for the Modale-Mondamin team (the Mud Ducks). It was a Saturday and we had a game in Woodbine. For some reason no one was available to take me to the game. A couple other guys on the team, including my buddy, Troy, needed a ride, too. What the heck, I decided I could get us there. So, I jumped into the Blazer with my bat, glove, and cleats and headed over to Troy's place out south east of Modale. I picked up Troy and couple other guys and off to Woodbine we went. The trip was about 25 miles one-way, with way too much of it on paved highways. But, we made it to the diamond in time for the game and without drawing any unwanted attention. I don't remember if we won or lost; the real excitement was during the return trip. We were just a mile from Troy's place, driving a little too quickly down the gravel road that passed in front of his house, when the truck suddenly started pulling pretty hard to the passenger side and was really difficult to control. I managed to stop without slipping into the ditch on the right side of the road. We got out, took a look around the truck, and found that we had had a blowout of the rear passenger side tire. And, for some reason, I had no spare. This predicament was a recurring theme throughout my teen years. Fortunately, Troy's older brother also drove a Chevy truck and let me borrow his spare to get home. I had some 'splainin' to do for that one. I think I only owned up to going to Troy's house but not to the full 60 mile round trip across the county. Not the smartest thing I ever did but still one hell of an adventure for a preteen.

By the time I turned 14 and could finally get a legal permit to drive (to school functions only, of course) I pretty much roamed the roads and highways in the "M Triangle" (Modale-Mondamin-Missouri Valley) with impunity. The first vehicle that was assigned for my use was not the Blazer but rather a black, 2-wheel-drive, 4-cylinder, 5-speed Ford Courier mini pick-up. My Grandpa Maule had taught how to drive a stick using this truck and since it could only carry three people (cramped) in the cab and would only exceed 75 miles per hour if going down a really steep hill it was deemed perfect for my use. The only things perfect about it were its ability to get 30 miles to the gallon and the ooo-gah horn gramps had installed.

The most memorable trip I ever made in that little truck was when I was 14 and milking my School Permit for all it was worth - and then some. It was one night after watching a West Harrison High School football away game (rode the "Spirit Bus" to and from the game) that the girl I obsessed over during my early teens and I went on a cross country drive to avoid going home too early on a Friday night. Mondamin to Onawa to Tekehmah, Nebraska to Blair, Nebraska to Missouri Valley to Modale and, finally, back to Mondamin. It was a shade over 145 miles since we never got onto Interstate Highway 29. A long 145 miles of very awkward silence since she knew I liked her a lot and I knew that she knew that I liked her a lot and I also knew she was totally not interested and was only with me because she couldn't drive yet. 25 years later and I still remember the trip and wouldn't trade the memory of that protracted, icy silence spent with her for anything.

I started driving the Blazer full time when I turned 16 and finally got a full-fledged drivers license. The rest has already been pretty well chronicled here.

Now, to quote the comedian Ron White, "I told you that story so I could tell you this one." Back in the day before my friend, Lloyd, met my neighbor, Mary Pat, he was a bit of a hooligan. Being of kindred spirit, one day when I was 15 he bequeathed to me a wondrous gift, something rare and powerful, something of questionable origin, something that had been passed to him from his brethren and had remained hidden for many years.

OK, enough hyperbole, he gave an archaic, red rotating police light his brother had swiped several years earlier. It needed light bulbs (the originals had been removed to use on a snowmobile) and it had no mount or wiring harness. The bulbs were easy to replace from the stock of snowmobile parts my Dad had left in our machine shed. I fixed the power problem by clipping the cigarette lighter end off the cord of an obsolete radar detector (one of those big square brown box ones that had a large yellow warning light and an obnoxious buzzer, both of which grew in intensity when near a radar gun, train crossing, automatic door, etc.) and connected it to the remnants of the power wires inside the emergency light housing.

The mount, though, was not as easy. Originally, I connected the light to a short piece of pipe (aircraft grade) and used stainless steal hose clamps to attach the pipe to the driver's side mirror of the Beast. I finished the jerry rigging of the light in the early part of '84. Since I was still in Drivers Ed, I only did a few test drives with everything attached and connected. I described my new toy to a few friends at track practice one day and one of them (one who had a license already) volunteered to drive the Beast so we could harass honest road faring citizens that coming Saturday. I will not divulge the name of the driver partly to protect his identity and mostly because I can't remember who it was.

The night started by leaving my house and heading south on Highway 127 towards Missouri Valley. The posted limit was 50 so by traveling at, well, way more than that, we caught up to our first prank-ee a few miles north of Mo Valley. The high speed was causing the light to list a bit but when I plugged in the power cord and it lit up and started rotating, the car in front of us immediately pulled onto the meager shoulder. And, we blasted right on past, laughing hysterically. We saw as we passed that we had pulled over a friend of ours from the Class of '85. That made us laugh even harder.

We skirted around the outside of Mo Valley, got onto Interstate 29, and headed back north. The light was listing a little worse but we still managed to get two more cars to pull over between Mo Valley and Modale. One turned out to be a girl I had known my whole life who went ballistic when she saw who it was: she already had a few tickets under her belt and thought this was the end of her driving privileges for a long while.

We were a bit surprised that people would stop for a blue and white POS Chevy Blazer but such is the power of the red light. Feeling that we had pressed our luck enough on such a busy road we took the Modale exit and headed west to our main quarry. There was going to be a keggar at the Dugdale farm out west of town. The smart thing would have been to show up and hoist a few with the fellows but we hadn't been formally invited. So, we were going to crash the party and do so by making a grand entrance.

We drove out to the party. I knew the noise made by the Beast's 454 big block bellowing through the burned out dual glass packs would give us away when we got close so when we pulled to within a quarter mile I plugged in the light and we raced to the pasture where the party was being held. As we pulled into the field we could still make out the forms of the attendees sprinting across the pasture towards the timber at the fence line.

They had left their trucks, cars, and, more importantly, the keg, tapper, and cups. We poured ourselves a lukewarm draught of Milwaukee's Best (or maybe it was Meister Brau) and laughed until they started carefully making their way back to the keg. We left before they got close enough to get too angry - and vengeful.

Having had more fun than teenagers ought to have in one night, we decided to head home. It was on the county road between Modale and Mondamin where we decided to use the light one last time. The light was listing so badly now that we had the driver's window rolled down and were holding it upright as we drove. As we neared a car about half way to Mondamin, I again plugged in the light. As had happened several times earlier in the night, the car slowed and pulled onto the shoulder. Only this time, our laughter was cut short as we blazed past the parked car. It could have been anyone else but instead the butt of our joke this time was our track coach – who was also the Drivers Ed instructor. I unplugged the light and we called the evening done.

That following Monday the party goers had decided that since they hadn't actually gotten arrested and since their keg and tapper had been left intact, it was actually kind of funny. They also decided not to kick the crap out of me (my not so inconspicuous truck had been recognized as we left), which was nice. In Drivers Ed, my instructor asked me how my weekend had been and suggested I might want to be more careful in the future. All things considered, that was a pretty cool response considering he probably didn't even know for sure that I wasn't driving my own truck that night.

I would like to note that as strong as my love-hate relationship was with the Beast, nearly every truck I have owned since then (I'm on my eighth truck now since the Beast) has had no resemblance to the Beast and have looked more like that black Courier in which Grandpa taught me how to drive.

"Imitation is the Sincerest Form of Flattery."
Charles Caleb Colton

I was talking to a recent West Harrison graduate who was telling me how she and her best friend had "the run of the school" their senior year. A few years ago I remember one of my cousins saying essentially the same thing. I imagine every year there are a few West Harrison Hawkeye seniors who believe that they rule the school. I won't go so far as to say I had total campus control but for much of 1985 and part of 1986 I did enjoy essentially free reign of the hallways.

The statute of limitations has probably run out by now so I can 'fess up. Besides, I did some time for this one so I guess double jeopardy allows me to come totally clean. I was once a forger. Actually, I was usually bored, so out of necessity I became a forger.

Study Halls were too quiet and too unproductive for my taste, so I chose to leave them at every opportunity. That was usually pretty easy; everyone knows that our band and choral director (also my great uncle), Bruce, would always oblige a request to come down to the Music Room to practice for whatever concert or contest that was coming next with a hall pass graced with his official "B. Norris" at the bottom (the last half of "Norris" was nigh-on illegible. One day I had forgotten to ask Bruce for a hall pass to escape Study Hall and was stuck. Or, was I?

I engaged the Study Hall monitor in a bit of witty, inane banter that was likely clever only to me. The quality of the repartee was immaterial; the verbal diversion allowed me to palm a book of yellow hall passes off the desktop. Back at a corner table in the Library I wrote myself a pass and scribbled a BNor-scrawl at the bottom. Not a very good likeness but I was desperate to escape.

A bit to my surprise it worked and I was free for the hour. Of course I actually went down to the music room - what the hell else is there to do in a 9 through 12 high school in a rural town of 400? But, I gained a new hobby: perfecting the BNor-scrawl and writing passes for myself - and for others needing temporary freedom.

After a bit of practice even Bruce couldn't tell my signatures from his own. Of course, he never really questioned how so many students ended up in his music room every day so there is a good chance he didn't really care that someone else was writing passes for him.

Once I became proficient with Bruce's John Hancock, I became bored with it. My handiwork was indistinguishable from the original - where's the thrill in that? So, I began working on others. I could do a passable Mr. Reichert (Guidance Counselor), a pretty good double "J" of the school secretary, but the one of which I was most proud was the principal's D. Penkert. I had it down cold.

I could only use D. Penkert's on rare occasions - the principal doesn't give out many passes. I was good and I knew it. My arrogance proved to be my undoing.

We had a substitute for several days in a class - a subject in which the sub readily admitted she knew very little. After the third day of no lecture and a short assignment of reading and problems to keep us busy, I got bored. Idle hands, devil, yada, yada, yada. So, on the fourth day I wrote myself a pass out of class.

I used the Bruce signature. In retrospect, maybe the principal's signature would have been a better choice. Sitting there, bored, would have been the wisest course of action, but instead I wrote myself a pass. Somewhere between the classroom and the Music Room a couple of intercom calls were made. Although the signature was flawless, the pass' purpose and validity came into question by the sub. By the time I got to the Music Room a new pass was waiting for me - to the principal's office. And, it wasn't one I had written.

Getting myself out of thirty minutes of boring class time got me into three hours of detention - my first and only detention ever. Of all the pranks I played, I ended up in detention only because a temp asked the main office why I needed to go to the music room. I considered myself lucky.

I finished out the remainder of our senior year using only real passes with authentic staff signatures. Side note: anyone interested in authentic autographed sports or movie memorabilia should visit my store on eBay – I'll even throw in an official looking Certificate of Authenticity.

"Take off, to the Great White North"
Take Off – Bob and Doug MacKenzie and Geddy Lee

Every day in high school at the end of 2nd period was the reading of the Daily Announcements. It was as regular as our friend, Flash the Gentle Giant, before a wrestling meet weigh-in. Often the announcements were banal and inconsequential with such tidbits of information as this from our last day of class on May 9, 1986: "Seniors: you may turn in locker padlocks during morning study halls or during lunch hour. If you lost it, you owe the office." Riveting.

Typed up in the morning by the school secretary, Mrs. Jungck, and distributed by trusted student office helpers at the start of second period, the one sheet (usually) of announcements were read aloud by the instructor in each classroom. The best part of the Daily Announcements weren't even heard; they were the confidential Faculty Announcements at the bottom of the page. Students weren't supposed to be privy to that information and the teachers were supposed to detach and dispose of that part of the page but it was always easy to find a sheet with them still intact. For instance, on May 13, 1985 the lone Faculty Announcement read "STaff [sic]: if any seniors failed a class for you for the 2nd semester, please inform me by 3:30 today. Hope this is not too much of a rush. Thanks, Mark" Ho-hum.

But, on 5/16/85 one of the two Faculty Announcements was "Attention faculty: please drop D--- M--- from your class rolls." confirming what many of us had heard: D--- had dropped out of school. Not earth shattering but interesting.

However, in the spring of our junior year there was a series of announcements that I thought was intriguing. On Tuesday, May 14, 1985, amongst the usual drivel in the Announcements, there was one that literally commanded my attention: "Attention: any high school 4-Hers interested in the Mapleleaf Canadian Trek please contact Floyd Perkins - 456-2938."

I was a 4-H'er. Sort of. I was very involved in 4-H during my pre-teen years and then sort of involved when I was in High School. On Wednesday, May 15, 1985, there was a follow-up announcement: "4-Hers--anyone interested in the Mapleleaf Canadian Trek sign up right away. Deadline is tomorrow. Call Floyd Perkins 456-2938 before tomorrow night." I hadn't called yet and thought it odd that this trip wasn't something I had heard about at the 4-H County Council meetings. Through some goofup, I was on the County Council.

Yes, somehow, even though I hadn't had an entry in the County Fair for years, I had managed to become treasurer of my local Club and appointed to the County Council along with my friend and mentor, Big Al.

Thursday, May 16, 1985, had yet another announcement about this trip: "4-Hers: remember, today is your last day to sign up for the Canadian Trek. Call Floyd Perkins at 456-2938. You must be 17 years of age."

Funny thing about the Daily Announcements back in our day: each day they started as just a blank sheet of paper on a clip-board on the secretary's counter in the principal's office; anyone could walk in and write almost anything on that piece of paper and it would be read. Anyone.

I studied several weeks' worth of announcement pages to see if it was possible to insert subliminal messages into the page vertically by carefully choosing the words of seemingly innocuous information but Mrs. Jungck. changed the margins on her typewriter so often that it couldn't be guaranteed from day to day to be the same.

On Friday, May 17, 1985, there was a final Canadian Trek message: "Floyd Perkins would like to say he's sorry for having to turn people down. Due to the influx of last minute calls, seats were limited. If you have questions, please call 645-2497 and ask for Marlin."

I was very surprised by this announcement because it was the only one I hadn't fabricated. Late Thursday (5/16) afternoon I had received an official Telephone Message slip taken in the principal's office. It stated that Floyd Perkins called for me and requested that I return his call; his message read "Glad to hear you are willing to co-sponsor our great Canadian Trek. Please call me back for further details!!!" You can't tell me Mrs. Jungck didn't have a sense of humor.

It was spring, near the end of the school year, and I was feeling prankish so I had penciled out a series of seven bogus announcements to insert into the mix of real announcements but Mrs. Jungck was on to me half way through the series. She wrote the 5/17 one on her own and sent me the phone message to let me know the jig was up. It wasn't like I was being overly clever with my messages but kudos to her for keeping with the spirit and playing along.

"Country Roads, Take Me Home"
Take Me Home, Country Roads – John Denver

When we were sophomores in high school a couple of senior guys got summer jobs working on the Harrison County Secondary Road Department survey crew. During the week they always showed for baseball practice about half an hour late because there is no direct route between the County Shop in Logan and the ball diamond in Pisgah. The stories of goofing off, screwing around, and occasionally working were enough to entice my friends, Mac and Lewey, and me to apply for similar positions when we became seniors. What a great plan. Too bad it didn't work out exactly according to plan.

Instead of being assigned to the survey crew we were given chainsaws and sent out to the county's back roads to rid the gravel roads right of ways of unwanted brush. Eight hours a day (15 minute breaks at 9am and 2:30pm and 30 minutes at noon for lunch) five days a week we cut sumac, black locust, wild plumb, cottonwood, birch, pine, cedar, walnut, and, once, I think, even a sequoia. And the refuse we ran through a massive wood chipper.

For the first few weeks the most interesting part of our job was seeing how big a chunk o' tree we could force through the chipper. That got old fast. We moved on to seeing what various objects did when sent through the chipper. Surprisingly, once you've seen a chipped Twinkie, the excitement of that game has peaked.

One afternoon during break one of the guys from the Woodbine shed started hitting rocks with a limb from a young oak we had cut up. From that simple act sprang forth a new break time (some breaks went a little long) activity of Stick-Rock Homerun Derby.

As we cut up brush we were on the lookout for a better "bat" and at lunchtime as we ate our meals sitting on the shoulder of the finest gravel roads in the west-central part of the great State of Iowa, we scavenged for smooth, semi-round rocks to hit. The chump of the day would don a hardhat and lob rocks to the batters who would have to hit said rocks past the nearest road sign to count as a homer. The one with the most homers at the end of break won. Won nothing tangible other than the admiration and respect of his peers. Line drives back at the pitcher were a bitch but still part of the game - hence the hard hat.

Surprisingly, I managed to escape injury while playing the game but did get a slight concussion when one of my fellow brush cutters managed to drop a 20-foot tall cottonwood on my noggin. I choose to believe it was an accident. I think Lewey and I once had the misfortune of dropping a tree on a car that had ignored our Brush Crew signs. I also accidentally took out power lines when a pine tree I notched fell the wrong way and crossed some overhead lines. What a pretty fire that was.

Eventually I was promoted from the brush crew to driving the roller on the road crew. Some of the full-timers didn't like that much (it's a union thing) but none of them liked driving the roller, either, and I was the only person who could drive it for eight hours straight without falling asleep.

Working on the road crew taught me a lot of things about road design and public works projects, knowledge I draw upon even today. How not to design, how not to use in-house labor, how not to construct, etc.

I did, however, get to work with some really great guys: Jim Pelton, Jim Clark, and Bill Hrabek come to mind, first and foremost. All good at what they did, patient enough to teach me the finer points of County work, and always willing to buy me a beer at the bar in Moorhead. It was because of that job and those guys that I can honestly say on my resume that I can drive a maintainer, dump truck with 2-speed axle, roller, sheep's foot, and anything with 3-on-the-tree transmission. Not proficient at any of them, but I can say with a straight face I have wheel time at them all.

Take, for instance, a small public works project I helped construct in the summer of 1987.

A bridge north of Pisgah had been deemed unsafe for loads heavier than a coconut-laden African swallow and was closed (the piece of crap bridge was failing after *only* 80 years of neglect). This caused problems for the farmers who routinely drove fully loaded grain trucks over it. To mitigate the several mile detour this necessitated, the County Engineer decided a new road should be built between the closed bridge and a slightly less dangerous bridge 1 mile to the north. Since there was no money budgeted for new road construction it was decided that County personnel would construct it using County equipment. Pisgah had the closest Harrison County Secondary Road Department shed so it was up to those of us who reported to said shed to build the road. "Us" being Jim Pelton, Jim Clark, Bill Hrabek, Jerry Hussing, and I.

Cocky from completing my freshman year of engineering at Iowa State, I asked the North Foreman, Art (a.k.a. "Unit 11" on the County radio system), a few basic questions about the new road's plans and specifications. Q: "How wide is the Right of Way easement?" A: "Don't need one; the farmer needs the road." Q: "How high will the grade be?" A: "High as we can get it." Q: "Where are the plan and profile drawings?" A: "Don't need any." And, lastly and most importantly since I would be running the sheep's foot and flat roller compactors, Q: "What are the compaction requirements?" A: "Beat the piss out of it." I'm pretty sure there was no kind of Environmental Assessment, Environmental Impact Study, or any other analysis of the havoc we were about to wreak on the hills, fields, and possible wetlands in the area. With that I was initiated into the art of road construction.

Bill drove an elevated grader and cut ditches for the new road, tossing the dirt ("soil" in engineering parlance) into the new roadbed. Jim Clark scraped more dirt off one of Iowa's Loess Hills near the failing bridge and Jim Pelton trucked it over to the roadbed and added it to Bill's efforts. Jerry used a maintainer to even out the "lifts" of dirt. And, I drove a vibrating sheep's foot roller over the roadbed, "beating the piss out of" the dirt until it was as hard as stone. I probably over compacted the soil but I hadn't had that class yet.

We worked for several days adding dirt on this new roadbed, raising it "as high as we could get it" between the riverbank and the relocated edge of the cornfield. It took maybe a week or so before we all noticed a slight problem with the new road. Although it was straight as an arrow and was connecting nicely with the existing roads, it was narrow. Way narrow. Too narrow.

Shit.

Well, Art noticed the narrowness, too. Of course he expected us to fix it. Easier ordered than done. I was thinking this wouldn't have happened if there had been a set of plans and specifications to follow but I kept that nugget of wisdom to myself.

Bill, Jerry, and the Jims set to bringing more dirt to the new road, dumping it along the narrow road's shoulders. They did this for about a day until the loose soil mounded up to the height of the narrow roadbed. Then I got back into the action, driving the sheep's foot along the shoulders, trying to compact the new dirt.

When we started the road, I was compacting the dirt as it was placed in layers of about 8 inches deep. No problem. But, now the road was nearly complete and the new dirt was basically two feet wide and about 6 feet high - on a slope, no less – and I was supposed to "beat the piss out of it" too. It wasn't really possible but orders are orders so I gave it a go. I think I managed to roll on the precarious edge for a couple of hours, making a few passes on both sides of the road before the inevitable happened: the new dirt gave way and my roller started to slide - and tip.

The Bomag sheep's foot I ran was articulated, bending behind the front compaction drum and in front of the cab. When it started to tip, I cranked the wheel and shut down the throttle and drum vibration. There I sat in the teetering piece of heavy equipment, bent like a gate hinge with its center pointing towards the new ditch and the drum and wheels under the cab clinging to the slope. The roller continued its teeter, even after I hastily shut it off and jumped clear. Who'd a thunk it? The sumbitch didn't roll. That's what Jim Clark said when he brought an end-loader over to try to pull it off the slope. Bill said the same thing when he brought a maintainer over to help the overtaxed end-loader. Oh, yeah, I was back on the roller driving it as the big iron pulled. Art told me "there's fuck-ups and there's fuck-ups" and that I needed to drive my own mess back onto the road. I wept at the showing of sympathy.

Eventually we got it back onto the roadbed - and decided that enough piss had been beaten from those new shoulders. Shortly after that a layer of gravel was added and the crummier of the two bridges was closed. As far as I know that narrow road with mushy shoulders is still being used.

"It's Money that Matters"
It's Money that Matters – Randy Newman

One the accomplishments of which I am the most proud is the obscene amount of money our class was able to raise. Prom decorations our junior year were the best that gymnasium had seen in many years.

Car washes, bake sales, extortion, and the resurrection of the school carnival enabled us to amass a balance of cash reserves that, quite frankly, worried the behoosips out of Principal Penkert. In addition to the dough from the carnival, which the school controlled, the cash-ola from the other fund-raisers went into a separate account our class treasurer opened for the class at the Mondamin Savings Bank.

In what I believe was a transgression of State and/or Federal banking laws, the school actually got the bank to tell them our account information and balance. I'm not sure which disappointed me more: that the principal did an end run around our class treasurer or that the bank gave up information about an account to a third party without a warrant or our permission. The account was moved to Missouri Valley shortly after that incident.

This is for my friends Danny (5/27/68 - 5/22/94), Preston (6/29/71 - 6/22/91), Tobi (6/2/68 - 11/23/82), and Dena (7/11/69 - 11/24/00). You expect the people with whom you grow up to always be there; their departure makes our crowded world seem a little too empty. I should have taken the time to talk to them more when I had the chance.

I talked with a friend in
my dreams last month
Eleven years have gone since he
passed away
It doesn't seem so long but there
were lots of things to tell him
It was good to talk again
"Remember the riding bikes
in the sand pits when we were kids?"
"Yeah, those were good times"
I forgot to ask if he knew why
he had to leave so soon

I talked to another friend in
my dreams last week
Fourteen years now since he

passed away
It's not all that long but he's
missed so much
It was nice to shoot the breeze
"Remember when we roared down the
road in my old truck?"
"Yeah, that was really cool"
I forgot to ask him why
he left so soon

A friend and I talked in
my dreams yesterday
It's been twenty-two years since
he passed away
It was just a short time ago but
so much has changed
I was glad to fill him in
"Remember when we did those
wheelies with your chair?"
"Yeah, that was a lot of fun"
I forgot to tell him I was sorry
he had to leave so soon

I visited a friend in
my dreams last night.
It was only hours before I knew
she had passed away.
So much remains
for us to talk about.
"Just wait until yours grows up
like you."
"She'll have a great life"
I didn't think to ask
not to leave so soon.

I wonder who will visit
my dreams tonight
So little time has passed
but there is so much of
what was
to talk about
I have to wonder
what might have been
if they hadn't left so soon.

Instead of the kegger the overly paranoid school officials expected us to throw with the money we earned, our class has now given out four scholarships in memory of our friends and classmates to graduates of West Harrison: one in 1986, one in 1996, one in 2001, and one in 2006.

"I awoke this morning with devout thanksgiving for my friends, the old and the new."
Ralph Waldo Emerson

A great deal of time has passed, but the memory of that weekend still remains fresh; it seems as though it was only a few days ago.

I'm not a big fan of the holidays. Thanksgiving signifies the start of a six-week stretch of time that is too busy, too commercial, and too stressful I think Lincoln's astute observation on deception and the public has an ancestral corollary that is best exemplified during the holiday season: You can get along with all of your family some of the time, you can get along with some of your family all of the time, but you can't get along with all of your family all of the time. More often than not my experience during those "special days" - the last six weeks each year - has been just getting along with some of the family some of the time (I really do need to try harder). This particular year started differently. It began with a calm, enjoyable Thanksgiving at the home of my in-laws, everyone getting along with everyone else.

The holiday tradition my wife and I endure is based on a marital compromise made early in our relationship. My parents live near Dallas, Texas (Oklahoma now); her parents live in Ames, Iowa. Her two sisters live in Cedar Rapids, Iowa; my sister lives in Dewey, Oklahoma; my brother lives in Austin, Texas. Her grandmother lives in a small town in eastern Iowa; my grandmother lives in a small town in western Iowa. Since our family map looks like a double-ought buckshot blast aimed at a map of the Mid-West, we decided during our first year together that we would not be driving all over middle America each holiday just to make an abbreviated cameo at each family's respective celebration. We adopted the "alternating plan": Thanksgiving is spent with one side of our family, Christmas with the other, and the following year the converse. This plan has been in place for fifteen years, and it still has not received complete acceptance from either side of our family. I believe that mutual dissatisfaction is the indicator of a fair plan.

Thanksgiving this particular year was with my wife's family in Ames, Iowa. I love the town of Ames. If the planets were to align properly and job opportunities for both my wife and I became available simultaneously, we would move there in a heartbeat. My wife grew up there, and both she and I got our Bachelor of Science degrees from Iowa State University, which is located near the heart of Ames. (Some of us believe it is the heart of Ames). She and I met in Ames, dated in Ames, and eventually got married in Ames. Though I only lived there for a little more than five years, Ames is almost like a second home to me. Our careers took my wife and I to Kansas City, but we made Lawrence, Kansas, our place of residence - because we found it to be a reasonable facsimile of Ames.

We made the four and one-half hour drive from Lawrence to Ames on Wednesday night. Snow flurries kept some of the less confident drivers home and a few of the less skilled drivers in the ditches. This cleared the path for the likes of me, which I greatly appreciated. The night before we left I made a compilation compact disc of obscure and irreverent Christmas songs (Blue Christmas sung by Porky Pig, Jingle Bells done in dog barks, Grandma Got Run Over by a Reindeer, and other such fare). The last thirty minutes of the disc contained the entire audio track of our favorite Christmas cartoon, How the Grinch Stole Christmas. We listened and laughed all the way to our traditional midway pit stop, the Qwik Trip in Bethany, Missouri. (It has grown a lot over the last fifteen years). We listened to most of it again (still funny) before finally rolling into the driveway of my in-laws' home at 10:34 p.m.

One of my sisters-in-law, Diane, and her fiancé, Lee, had arrived. I was beat from the drive and after verifying that A) I was fine (mostly true), B) the cat still had a pleasant personality (still fat), and c) my job remains a vacuous endeavor (still sucks), I retired for the evening. My better half stayed up into the wee hours of the morning talking family matters. Christmas for this half of our family was to be celebrated the next day, Thanksgiving. It was my intention to be well rested for Santa.

I believe football was created to promote family harmony during the holidays. The Cowboys and Lions put a stranglehold on the male (and, to a certain extent, female) attention span every Thanksgiving. For that, I am thankful. My father-in-law, Gene, is both a retired attorney and retired college instructor; my brother-in-law, John, has a Ph.D. in mathematics and is an honest-to-gosh rocket scientist; my future brother-in-law, Lee, is in marketing and sales; my nephew, Jay, only ten (too old to convince to run in circles until puking sick, too young to tell/hear crude jokes); my mother-in-law, Rosemary, is a retired college advisor; my sister-in-law, Karen, is a former CPA and full time parent; Diane is a computer network developer; my wife's grandmother, Oma, is in her eighties and grew up in the communal Amana colonies, and my niece, Sarah, is only eight and suffers from the same limitations as her brother, Jay. We have little in common, but, we all like to watch football (well, Oma and Sarah don't, but we expect Sarah to come around when she gets older) and the traditional two Thanksgiving NFL games divert our attention from any meaningful conversation for nearly eight hours, the only interruption is the turkey dinner.

The mood this year was different. It may have been because Gene and Rosemary had recently retired and had less stress in their lives. It may have been because Jay and Sarah are getting older and are in that transition from rambunctious children to surly teenagers. Perhaps it was because this was the first year that Diane's ex-husband was not in attendance (and, therefore, not grating on everyone's nerves). Or, maybe it was because I'm mellowing. Things seemed different; calmer, more relaxed, not at all unpleasant.

By evening the turkey was eaten and the football games were finished, so we exchanged Christmas gifts on Thanksgiving Day. The kids and I got several toys (I've been told I am difficult to shop for). I was too busy playing to notice what everyone else got. After all the presents were opened and I had thrown my last scrap of wrapping paper at Diane, discussion of the next bi-annual day-after-Thanksgiving shopping spree began. I tried to tune this out – I don't like large, unruly crowds. The main objective of this shopping foray was to buy the many computer related items at prices too good to be true at Office Depot. I tried in vain to point out that because this was a college town, moreover, a technically oriented college town, a mob of pocket protector clad techno-nerds would bound to be charging the store. The mob was probably camping outside the store: an information age, Woodstock-esque gathering with stories of hard drive failures and website hacks traded while large quantities of Jolt Cola were consumed. The family dismissed my concerns as the rant of a paranoid agoraphobic. Perhaps they were correct; however, while they shopped, I intended to sleep.

I then discovered that Diane, Lee, Karen, John, Oma, and the kids were all going to return to Cedar Rapids Friday afternoon; this was two days sooner than I had expected. Ordinarily I may not have minded this. I had intended to visit campus, read a book or two, and, time permitting, go pheasant hunting with a friend. But, it was so enjoyable up to this point that I was going to forego some of my plans to spend more time with the family. I felt a bit disappointed that it was going to end so soon. Of course, I was still going to sleep through what would assuredly be an unmitigated melee at the stores – rabid dogs could not chase me into a store the day after Thanksgiving. I did capitulate without resistance to meeting everyone for lunch at Hickory Park, the best bar-b-que restaurant in the Mid-West.

I awoke late Friday morning to the raised voices of disgruntled shoppers returning vanquished from Office Depot and other stores unnamed. I hinted around the "I told you so" phrase but refrained from saying it outright. I thought someone mumbled that I had been correct in my prediction but I may have just imagined it. I enjoyed the moment just the same.

Lunch was outstanding, as usual (I highly recommend Hickory Park – it's on South Duff in Ames). Good-byes were traded and, what was to me all too soon, the Cedar Rapids family members departed for home. My wife, her parents, and I remained in the quiet. The quiet that I usually wish for had arrived, but I found myself bored. Go figure.

A friend (and co-worker) also has in-laws near Ames; he, too, was up from Kansas City for Thanksgiving. Weeks earlier we had made tentative plans to go pheasant hunting the Saturday after Thanksgiving. Now that everyone had gone home, I gave him a call to see if he was still interested. He was in a small house with many in-laws, big and small, and was eager to get out for a morning. He would provide transportation, location, and a dog, three of the five most important elements of a successful morning of pheasant hunting. The forth and fifth are, of course, birds and prowess with a shotgun, neither of which can be guaranteed. All I had to do was show up.

With all the lack of activity in the house, I decided to go to bed early Friday night. I had a pretty mean case of indigestion – maybe from the bar-b-que lunch, maybe from the Pizza Pit pepperoni pizza for supper, maybe from the seven or eight Diet Mountain Dews I'd had in less than twelve hours. The cause was irrelevant; the effect was a very restless sleep with bizarre dreams. I have forgotten all but the last one. I was back in high school with several of my classmates. Paul F. was in the dream, even though he had moved while we were in junior high. There was Teresa B. and John F. and Troy B. and, well, there were a lot of them in my dream. And, they were all spies, just as I was. We didn't know who was on whose "side." We all were carrying pistols. Lots of shots were being exchanged, most of them fired at me – I guess they didn't like the ten-year reunion that I had planned. I tried to defend myself but in Nightmare on Elm Street type irony, I could not get my pistol to fire. There is nothing like being chased and shot at by an angry gang of spying classmates through a high school building (a building that subconsciously I knew had been demolished five years ago) to get your heart rate accelerated. I finally managed to get the trigger on my gun to operate just as my alarm clock started to chirp. I awoke to discover that I had slept on my arm funny and had cut off circulation to my hand. Of course I had trouble pulling the trigger in my dream – it took four minutes of wake time before I could even feel my fingers. The dream was unsettling enough that it is still pretty clear in my memory. It probably always will be.

I managed to shower, wake up, and pull on my blaze orange hunting ensemble, more or less in that order. I left the house shortly after 7:05 a.m., which should have given me plenty of time to find my friend's mother-in-law's house. Our day was to begin at 8:00. At precisely 8:07 I pulled into the driveway. I was late, which I detest. My friend was up and ready. The dog and his owner (my friend's brother-in-law) however, had not arrived. Since his brother-in-law was actually providing the dog, the truck we would be riding in, and the property on which we would be hunting, I decided he could be as late as he wanted.

The day was cold, overcast, and windy. Not unbearable, not quite miserable, just not ideal. The weather turned out to be irrelevant. I loaded three shells of 7½ shot into my 12-gage Mossberg shotgun at sometime around 8:30. Three hours and several miles (by foot) later I ejected those same three shells back out of my gun and put them back into their box. We saw nothing all morning. Some would consider this a failed day of hunting. I disagree with that assessment. For me it was a moral success – I had not missed a shot all day.

We returned to the house, and I thanked my fellow hunters for allowing me to walk with them on this cold, windy day. We agreed that next time we would try walking through some fields that actually contained pheasants.

I got into my truck and started to drive back to my in-laws' house. My cell phone had a voice mail message on it from my wife asking me to call her – apparently shopping on this day had not gone well either. I called. She said she was wondering when I would be back, and she would talk to me then. For this I burned a couple of minutes of cell phone airtime.

So, I continued driving towards the house. I talked myself into taking a detour through the Iowa State campus to reassure myself that no other campus landmarks had been demolished since my last visit. I stopped and took some photos of my old dormitory and the windows out of which some hooligans had once launched oranges using a catapult made of surgical tubing and a crude denim pouch. I recalled the oranges traveled about 300 feet over the street and splashed down in Lake Laverne. Bananas don't fly as far. After I had nostalgia'd enough, I finished the drive back to the house.

I pulled into the driveway and crawled out of my truck; I was a dirty, sweaty, oxymoron of camouflage and blaze orange. I thought I would take a shower and a nap and then maybe take another nap. A mostly empty house does have its advantages. My wife heard me drive up and came out of the house to meet me in the driveway. She gave me a hug and started to cry.

That Saturday morning I learned how much technology has shrunk our world. I had purposely kept our home phone number unlisted in a futile attempt to thwart those vile and repugnant violators of personal privacy, telemarketers. In spite of this impediment, it only took less than an hour that morning for three different people to find and call my in-laws' house - call before 7:45 a.m. – looking for me. The network of my family and the closest of high school friends found me that day, a testament to how close people from a small community are and remain even when they move away. My grandmother, my mother, and a good friend from high school stayed on the telephone lines that day until they reached my in-laws because they wanted to be sure that I was notified by people who cared that another good friend, an old friend, and member of the West Harrison Class of 1986, Dena Globe, had died in a car accident just a few hours earlier.

Thanksgiving is still a sad time for me, but I choose to give thanks for the wonderful family and friends who have blessed my life.

"I kinda changed my direction, I guess I went and broke the family tradition"
Family Tradition – Hank Williams, Jr.

Something I don't see as much here in the 'burbs as I do when I travel back home is the graduation tassel a hangin' from the rear view mirror of a teenager's car. I see lots of bead necklaces (I don't want to know) and dreamcatchers but tassels, not so much. Maybe that's more of a rural thing or maybe it's just something that, like Wham! and Flock of Seagulls, didn't survive the 80's. Tradition.

I mentioned to someone down here that we turned our class rings so the year faced the right when we graduated - "out when you're out" - she said I was nuts. Then I said how some girls would put wax or string inside their boyfriend's ring so they could wear it on their left ring finger instead of putting it on a chain. Again, she called me loopy. Tradition.

One of the first times I took my (then soon to be) wife back home to meet my family we happened to be behind a pick-up truck that was just leaving the new high school, a young man at the wheel and a young lady sitting by his side. My wife mentioned how she hated that and would never sit by me like that. When I get a pick-up now, I opt for bucket seats - no sense in getting a bench seat. I remember when my high school girlfriend sat by my side I was on cloud nine. It was just one of those things that was done when you had a steady. Tradition.

When I last visited back home I saw that the Class of 2008 had spray painted their graduation year on the granary on the south end of Kelly Lane, as had been done by several other classes since the 1970s. Someday I hope someone from their class will explain why they had to cover the entire side of the building unlike all the other classes. Tradition.

My high school graduation tassel hangs on a small wooden stand on top of my computer at home. The black and white one, I mean. For eight years it had been in a cardboard box with my varsity letters and medals (I never bothered to get a letterman's jacket). Also on that stand is my college tassel, a bright orange shock of yarn that is just ugly enough to represent the college of engineering. The third tassel that hangs from the clip is my favorite even though it is very faded from years of hanging from the rear view mirror of the Beast (before the mirror fell off). It is a maroon and gold souvenir tassel, one I special ordered when we ordered caps and gowns and other shtuff for high school graduation (like Senior Keys, Memory Books, and

Graduation Announcements - the Jostens cartel is quite thorough). I don't know if I ever really explained to everyone why I had pushed for our class colors to be maroon and gold: it was a nod to the people like my dad who had been a part of or graduated from the Modale High School whose school colors were maroon and gold; trying to keep some traditions alive.

**"So hold on loosely,
Just don't let go"**
Hold on Loosely - .38 Special

I was addressing an email and saw an address I will never again have an opportunity to use. Everyone in my life is special in his or her own way. I realize today that you never really think about it until the opportunity has passed. This is for my friend Dena.

Dena was my first "steady" girlfriend in the fifth grade. She was a pretty blond and one half of a set of twins. Girlfriends up to this point were just childish relationships - the girl you slugged in the shoulder the most and maybe ignored more pointedly than the other girls.

But, fifth graders got to attend fifth and sixth grade dances that were occasionally thrown at the old Legion Hall. It wasn't mandatory to have a significant other to attend but not many attended stag so you really needed to bring your own dance partner.

So, after the requisite note passing and "check this box if you'll be my girlfriend" being checked in the affirmed, Dena was my first girlfriend, and accordingly, my date to my first boy-girl dance. We met at the Hall, of course; that's just how fifth grade dates were: you were taken there by your parents and you left with your parents and your "date" was the time in between.

It was a Christmas dance, that first one, where there were chips and punch and crappy post-disco techno-pop music. And, there was a sprig of mistletoe strung up in a secluded corner of the dance floor. Dena gave me my first real kiss at that dance under that mistletoe.

Like most pre-junior high romances, our courtship only lasted a few weeks, a few kisses. I can't say I remember them all but I do remember the excitement and anticipation of trying to steal a few moments for her kiss. Much as our "relationship" began, it ended with a check-box marked "no."

Twelve year olds are resilient: our next significant other was only a note-pass and check-box away; I'm relatively certain that Dena helped me draft my next "check-here-to-be-mine" tome. We finished elementary school, junior high school, and finally high school together, never "dating" again after fifth grade, but always remaining friends.

Like so many of my other high school friends, I fell out of touch with Dena when I left for college and never really talked to her much until our tenth high school reunion. We exchanged email addresses then and ever since I have sent her all manner of jokes, puzzles, and other electronic junk that everyone gets. And, in kind, she sent me pictures of her new daughter, heartwarming stories, and inspirational poems.

I feel so empty now, seeing how I squandered the chance to tell her anything of substance. I've always thought by forwarding humor to others that I might be putting a smile of their face. Now, I don't feel I've really accomplished that much at all.

"Our Next Speaker is Angie"

A few years ago my classmate, Angie, forwarded an email to me. It was one of those chain emails demanding that the recipient forward it to several people to keep the story alive. It was about a jock who helped a nerd pick up his books that some bullies had knocked out of the nerd's hands thus starting a friendship that lasted until their graduation. The nerd/valedictorian then confessed in his graduation speech that he was thinking of ending his life when the jock befriended him and showed him things weren't so bad after all.

I don't usually reply to this kind of message. They are usually works of fiction or recycled urban legends. I actually looked through several myth and hoax databases to find some verification that the speech was never actually given; I found no evidence to disprove it. This story bothered me then and still bothers me to this day. I have received it several times and have always deleted it. But, when it came from Angie, I felt it was just too ironic to not reply. She and I had given speeches at our graduation.

It took me nearly half a year to respond because though I thought of it daily, I was never able to put together the words to fully articulate how it compared to my memories of our graduation day and the speech I gave.

I still have my speech - the version of it that the school secretary, Mrs. Jungck, typed, that is. It's still in my Senior Memory Book next to our Commencement Program. I think she put my original hand written draft in the round file. What a transparent ruse that was. We all had taken either Typing I or Personal Typing and could have easily typed the speeches ourselves but the Principal "graciously" offered the services of his secretary to type up the final draft. Like we didn't realize that they just wanted to ensure that nothing controversial would be said. I was a little ticked at this because I actually liked to type. The whole semester I had of typing I always tried to sit in front of my friend, Missy, so I could attempt to keep pace with her typing. I would listen to her IBM Selectric pounding out characters and try to make my fingers match the speed of hers. It was only a couple of years ago that I confessed to her that she was my keyboard role model and that, because of her, I managed to bang out around fifty-five words a minute. So, the only copy of my old speech that I have is the double spaced text that was pre-approved and typed by someone other than myself. C'est la vie.

What I had been thinking since I received the message from Angie was not so much what I had said that day - I don't recall saying any of the words - but more so of some of the things that happened and how certain scenes from our graduation still replay clearly in my mind. I remember the rehearsal that we had a few days before graduation when we practiced walking into the gym, blocked out how we would move to the stage and back to our seats for the choral numbers, how the presentation of the scholarships would be done, and, finally, how we would receive our diplomas. Mac, Angie, and I stayed and went through our speeches at the podium on the stage once for practice. I understand they still use the same old, rickety, white plywood stairs to get up to the stage from the gym floor. I think it's still the same walnut stained podium with "W-H" on the front, too. We speakers were given just one instruction: "after you finish your speech introduce the next speaker." Pretty simple.

"Without Dreams There is No Tomorrow." Reading it now only takes about 93 seconds. Not very poignant or memorable, nothing to evoke an emotional response. But, I remember being near tears when I finished and leaving the stage without introducing Angie. As I spoke about starting school in Kindergarten and how we matured throughout our school years, developing friendships and relationships that at that time I was certain would last forever, I was thinking we were one student short at this graduation.

Tobi and I - and others, as well - used to argue about what pick-up was the best: Ford or Chevy (nobody drove a Dodge when we were kids). It was almost as heated a debate as the John Deere versus International Harvester conflicts. Heck, we were little kids; our favorite truck was the one our Dad drove. I was staunch Chevy supporter until Dad broke with tradition in 1982 and bought a Ford. Tobi was always a Ford man. Now that I look back on it it seems sad that of the three or four most vivid memories of him from the ten years I knew him, the bickering over a stupid truck always comes to mind first. What's even more ironic is that since striking out into the real world I owned four different brands of pick-ups: Isuzu, Mazda, Dodge, and Toyota, before breaking down and getting a GMC. The GMC was a compromise - maybe if I don't ever get a Ford or Chevy the argument will never be settled.

Anyway, as I was talking about how tomorrow doesn't happen without dreams, I was thinking how Tobi should be there with us. I saw his mom, Marlene, in the crowd. My speech was quite trivial when compared to the big picture of real life. It was an exciting day - the most important day of our lives to that point - and all of the sudden it seemed a little empty. I don't recall giving my speech at the podium but I remember walking back to the edge of the stage where Angie was standing and somebody said something about not doing the introduction. And then my memory was blank until we all were standing on the gymnasium floor in front of the stage after the ceremony had concluded, greeting our friends and family as new graduates. Even though we had all agreed we would throw our caps into the air, we chickened out just like every other class before us. I had my prescription mirrored shades on - "too cool for school," right? I was back to being pretty chipper at this point. Then Marlene came through the line and shook my hand. I didn't feel all that cool any more and had to take my sunglasses off. I think she knew what had been going through my mind on stage. Ironically, she thanked me for being a friend of Tobi's. I was thinking I hadn't been enough of a friend when the chance was there. I still see her at events when I go back home and she always makes it a point to talk to me. It saddens and angers me that muscular dystrophy took her son – my friend, *our* friend –from us far too soon. I still never know what to say to her.

I guess that's why I still search the 'net for proof that the email story Angie sent me is fiction. I was not able to change my friend's future. All I could do was talk of the future but think of him in the past tense. I spoke at the National Honor Society Induction Ceremony a few years ago. The theme of that speech was leading by example: "You never know who might be watching or what they may see." It's the little things that people remember: saying "Thank you," an unsolicited "I love you," holding open a door, or, maybe even the acknowledgment that Ford really does make a pretty decent pick-up truck.

I have a good friend, Soomi, who said to me once "You are a very nostalgic person." I guess she was surprised at how many stories I remembered from grade school, junior high, and high school. I just believe that no one should be forgotten.

What I have learned is that one needs to take a personal inventory of the special people in his or her life. Take a few seconds to let those friends and family know that they are important to you and that your life wouldn't be the same without them having been in it. If I had that podium again, that would be my speech. Say "thank you for being my friend" now because tomorrow that opportunity may not be there.

"Oh Maybelline, why can't you be true?"
Maybelline – Chuck Berry

My student government career began as high school Junior Class President in 1984. It was a position I actually wanted because the junior class was responsible for raising the money that would be used for paying for the Junior-Senior Prom and whatever was leftover would go towards graduation. I think we did pretty darn well in the fundraising department though after our last scholarship check our class account is now less than one Jackson from being zero (hint hint Class of '86).

My senior year allowed me the chance to be Student Council President, the highlight of which was being on the school lunch menu committee. Oh, and speaking at graduation, but I've already written about that disaster.

All this experience was grooming for my service as a Government of Student Body Senator at Iowa State University (elected twice). I have very fond memories of taking part in a government that few knew existed representing people who didn't care about things that meant little to the pursuit of higher education.

I would have never been a GSB Senator if not for my friend, Alan. He had held the same position as Senator for the residence hall in which he (and later, I) lived and convinced me to run for his seat when he "retired." It was supposed to be a "fun" diversion from my pursuit of a degree. It had its moments. Mr. Smith's assertion that Robert's Rules of Order is NOT a bag of tricks was dispelled quickly. Move to table the notion.

Part of being in the campus GSB was also being a part of my residence hall executive council. Oh, if only it were as cool as it sounds. Actually, there were several events, almost none of which were governmental-ish, that were cool. The cookouts we did for the residents during Spring move-in, the Terrace Room parties in South Friley Hall, and the DEBASH celebration, all of which were social events and all of which were probably the most useful things student government did for the masses. Goodness knows the office hours each week were an unnoticed waste.

To fulfill a Department of Residence requirement the executive council had to sponsor and/or present an educational program each semester. Most were quite forgettable; I can assert this because I have forgotten them all.

Except for one. My final semester as a member of the council, we sponsored an all-day slate of mini-sessions. I don't recall the theme that tied all the sessions together; I only remember the one session in which I actively participated. "Understanding the Opposite Sex." Like that could be explained in just an hour.

It was a very well attended session. It was a panel discussion with the panel comprised of three men and three women. Any three of each gender in the session could be on the panel. In fact, the only way to participate - speak, if you will - is if you were seated at the front of the room. It was run like a huge tag-team match: a person would say her or his piece and then would tag-off with someone (of the same gender) in the audience and then the new panelist would be free to opine to the group. Surprisingly, a lot men and women had a great deal to say about the opposite sex.

Also, though not as surprisingly, I spent a great deal of time at the front of the room representin' the X-Y. Over the years I have learned a thing or two about tweaking, button pushing, and generally annoying the heck out of others so, for me, this was like shootin' fish in a bucket. During the discussion on "respect" I dropped a few "chicks" and "babes" which, I must admit, garnered quite an impassioned response. A reference or three to cooking and ironing shirts further stoked emotions. Salmon in a shot glass.

The part of the discussion I recall most vividly had to do with the disparity in preparation time each gender needed before leaving for a night out. The general consensus was the fairer sex required considerably more time than the gents. I had to tag my way back onto the panel for this. One of the distinguished ladies from Helser Hall posited that women possibly took a wee bit more time for personal preparation because (at that time in the late 1980's) only women wore make-up, something that men (again, at that time in the late 1980's) did not do and could not understand. Besides, women only wear make-up for the benefit of men anyway, so we should just shut the heck up about taking so long to get ready.

Oh, really? Well, I guess...

..."IF THE BARN NEEDS PAINTING, THEN PAINT IT."

I remember thinking "wow, did I really say that out loud?" A quick glance around the room, half of which was cheering and the women looking as pissed as Jane Fonda at a VFW convention confirmed that I had indeed verbalized my thought. One of my (former) female friends from Rowe House threw a fellow woman out of one of the panel chairs so she could offer a very voluminous rebuttal. I think it was a rebuttal, I don't know, I wasn't really listening.

OK, I admit it. The line wasn't mine. It went over big, made me a hero of sorts with chauvinist pigs in the room. But, it wasn't mine.

The same man who told me the joke that had "Two obese Pattys, Special Ross, Lester Cheese pickin' his bunions all on a Sesame Street bus" as a punch line also once said "If the barn needs painting, paint it." I thought that was so freakin' funny I filed it away in my noggin for a day when I could bust it out. *Bust* it out. Ha! I'm unstoppable.

He had driven me and the rest of the 1984 Southwest Iowa Honor Marching Band to Dallas, Texas to march in the Cotton Bowl parade. He also encouraged me to get my first job with the Harrison County Secondary Road Department. He was the first Democrat for which I ever voted. On a sub-zero day in December of 1990 he, his son, and I emptied a diesel engine fuel filter into a sink in Hutton House in South Friley Hall. That same day we learned my four-cylinder Isuzu pick-up didn't have the umph to jump-start a car's V-8 diesel, even with ungelled fuel filters. I will always think of him as being one of the best county supervisors ever to serve Harrison County.

"If the barn needs painting, paint it."

I am going to miss Duane Grooms.

"I'm Wanted Dead or Alive"
Dead or Alive – Bon Jovi

Life with a price on its head is not easy. Nearly twenty years of life on the lam have passed. I had no clue how prescient those poets of pop and roll would be. At the time we all thought the big-haired bums of Bon Jovi were just another one-hit-wonder band and would last about as long as the flavor of a piece of Bubblicious gum (strawberry flavor). Of course, after the Mission, my life – our lives - became that song.

Well, not the cowboy part - I do two-step on occasion, but I live in the 'burbs and drive a Toyota. Not really the steel horse part either I haven't been on a bike since I took a 750 Hondamatic out for a spin the summer after the Mission. And, I guess they want us "alive" but that's just speculation on my part. But, we ARE still wanted; it's just a matter of time before we are hunted down and vengeance is exacted.

Everyone knows everything about everybody else; such are the checks and balances of a small community. Even so, names used are the codenames used by our team. I don't even remember whose idea it was; mine, maybe, but the inspiration was derived from many sources. "Hollywood" would be the simple answer; though it would be wrong of me to blame the industry that has provided so much joy and diversion to three increasingly violent and dysfunctional generations.

Now, I'm not implying that Hollywood's hypocritical holier-than-thou producers, writers, directors, and outspoken actors are necessarily a bad influence on the young and impressionable. How could I criticize an industry that has enabled me to avoid reality by watching fantasy worlds where the good are impeccable marksmen; the bad are incompetence personified; and perfect couples always blissfully ride off into the sunset. When Kenny, an upperclassman, broke his foot while trying to jump from one pick-up to another (at 50 miles per hour), I knew that if he hadn't just seen this act of adolescent machismo performed in the movie Footloose a person of his intellect and judgment would certainly have found another way to injure himself. It was inevitable. Anyway, he didn't complete the jump and crawled away from the stunt with valuable experience and knowledge and a deeper appreciation for Kevin Bacon's acrobatic prowess (he does his own stunts, right?). I saw that cinematic masterpiece as well, and it never occurred to me to take dad's Farmall M out and play an extremely slow motion game of chicken with a neighbor. Hell, even in road gear it would have taken us the better part of a day just to get two tractors close enough to see one another, let alone drive at each other. My great-uncle might argue that I would have never gone "surfing" through the middle of town on the roof of my truck had I not seen Michael J. Fox do the same in "Teen Wolf." Perhaps.

But, the Mission did not originate in Hollywood. To the best of my recollection, it was the culmination of years of frustration in the inequity of cable television availability in rural areas. This became excruciatingly clear during a party at Rudy's place late one Saturday night. We were, appropriately enough, watching television. Rudy's folks were out of town for the weekend. By default, his place became our rally point for that Friday night.

Rudy had a satellite dish. I don't mean one of the little eighteen-inch things that everyone seems to have strapped onto the south end of their homes these days. He had an old-school dish. Nine feet in diameter, made of black steel mesh, motorized to aid in scanning the heavens for additional satellite signals, capable of bringing raw TV signals directly into the home. It was a godsend for anyone dwelling in a statistically insignificant Nielson market. Or, it was until Ted Turner and his ilk began force-feeding their broadcasts into mainstream America using RG-6 cable. That urban American televisions were being connected to a coaxial IV drip wouldn't normally concern those of us in the rural heartland. We really didn't care. Until, that is, the signals Rudy's dish was tapping became scrambled. It wasn't enough to fleece the city people for the privilege of receiving shoddy installation, poor service, and a level of reliability akin to a Lucy and Ethel plan. No, those bastards had to deprive those of us in fringe markets of MTV.

Anyway, it was a Friday night in late summer of 1984. Rudy was again playing the role of gracious host, providing sanctuary and a current channel guide in exchange for Milwaukee's Best and Pizza Hut pan pizza (pepperoni with extra cheese). I had finished not playing well in a baseball game; it appeared that the serving of refreshments had begun: Rudy was messing with the dish controls. His cousin, Sarge, standing in the middle of the living room, was massaging the top of his head as he pulled a long drink out of a MB can. The ghetto blaster was playing Billy Squier so loud that I could almost not hear Rudy swearing at the hiss of static emanating from the television. A few empties were strewn about the floor. A half full pizza box was sitting open on the couch.

"What the hell is wrong with your head?" I asked Sarge while I started looking for a beer. Judging by the number of empties on the floor I knew I had to act quickly before the others arrived. I had another twelve-pack in my truck that could wait until supplies in the house dwindled - if that occurred.

"Rudy bet me my head wouldn't reach the ceiling fan if I stood on my toes."

Rudy and his family lived in what today is called a "pre-manufactured home." The ceiling was at best eight feet high. The ceiling fan hung down below seven feet.

"How much did he bet you?" I asked the 6'-2" Sarge.

"A beer."

Sarge was going into the Air Force when he graduated.

"Who brought the beer?" I asked.

It was easy pickin's for the recruiter when he walked in.

"I did," he said.

He was a good kid, usually did what he was told.

"So, he bet you one of your own beers that you could not stick your head in the ceiling fan?" I didn't really have to ask that but it seemed like the right thing to do.

He nodded as he finished his beer; I nearly wept for my country.

I didn't need to see the wobbling fan to see who "won" the bet.

I went to help Rudy with the TV. It was a piece of electronics equipment and the Y-chromosome in me required that I assist. Miami Vice was over (thank the maker) and Rudy had switched on the 'dish. He was scanning the skies for a satellite that still carried unscrambled "art" films. It was tedious work sifting through dozens of channels of scrambled static. The Milwaukee's Best didn't seem to help our tuning abilities.

Hendrix and Cookie showed up just as another staccato burst of fan blades against Sarge's noggin erupted. Sarge was checking to make sure the first time wasn't just a fluke. So, there were the four of us, Rudy, Cookie, Hendrix, and me, huddled about the dish controls, bickering about which bird was likely to have unscrambled skin. Our efforts were occasionally interrupted by the whap-whap-whap sound made by Sarge standing on his toes and sticking his head back in the fan. We never once broke the Code of Guy and checked the channel guide. It took nearly twenty minutes but we finally found a low quality show starring Miles Long and Becky Eezee (or some such ilk) with a soundtrack that was apparently done on a Colecovision.

We opened fresh beverages and started ridiculing the weak plot when the picture slowly faded to static. A chorus of cursing erupted, drowning out the fan blades whacking Sarge's head again - he had jumped up in anger and had another cranial incursion with the fan. Squid walked into the house and asked what the problem was; asked with a half smirk, asked in the sort of "I know what the problem is" way. Hendrix, Cookie, and I scrambled to the dish controls - the film had reached a critical point in the plot, and we wanted to restore the picture before clothing returned. Rudy ignored the TV and the controls and instead ran outside, punching Squid in the arm on the way. A minute later the men and women on Rudy's TV were doing what we had once thought Rudy returned holding something behind his back.

"Here's your hat, you page," he said, whipping a Farmer's CoOp hat at Squid's head.

That was an insult of the greatest magnitude. There had been a scandal in the state legislature involving some congressmen taking indecent liberties with a few of the congressional pages. Being called a "page" was a high order put-down.

The rest of us laughed our keesters off. The insult not withstanding, the practical joke was brilliant both in simplicity and in effectiveness. Squid had hung his hat on the receiving horn of the satellite dish, blocking the signal, and disrupting Debbie as she was working her way through Dallas. Rudy and Squid tussled for a few more minutes while the rest of us returned our attention to the flesh-tones gyrating on the television in front of us. The rest of the night was pretty uneventful; Sarge eventually had enough liquid personality in him that he would stick his head back into the ceiling fan. When the novelty of that stupid human trick wore off and the beer ran out, we all thanked Rudy for the splendid evening, still laughing at the "good-one" pulled by Squid. We headed for our respective homes (except for Sarge, who had passed out on the couch near the ceiling fan).

That was a pretty typical summer night for us. We were a pretty tight group. Our community was pretty small. Half of us called Mondamin our home, the other half considered Modale home. The truth of the matter was that Rudy lived in Mondamin and Cookie lived in Modale. The rest of us lived out in the country among the corn and soybean fields. Like it really mattered. Modale only had a population of 206 with a post office, a beauty shop, a library (open twice a week), one bar, and the town's largest employer, the Farmer's CoOp. Mondamin was only slightly better with a population of 411 and in addition to the accouterments of Modale, a flower shop, a sparsely stocked hardware store, and a grocery store. Oh, and the Mondamin Library was open three times a week. With such a limited selection of entertainment venues, it was only natural that television was a large staple of the free time diet. So, logically, there was a fair amount of life imitating art, e.g., Kenny Black.

It would be unfair to describe us as a group of Square Pegs. We were more like the Black Sheep Squadron. We did all the sports, participated in most community activities, did well in studies; and when things went a little too sedate, we raised a little havoc. Sometimes life has to take a swipe at art.

In that vein we first performed an act of community policing. Perhaps we were inspired by the opening credits of Miami Vice, maybe we were overreacting to a blatant disregard for aesthetic sensibility, or it could be we were venting frustration because the library was closed on a Saturday night. Whatever the case, something snapped one Saturday night, and we took action. It wasn't organized enough to be considered a Mission though many of the Mission's players were involved. It was more of a vigilante act. Though I'm probably just blocking, I don't recall whose idea this was either. It may have been Squid, or Hendrix, or me. It doesn't matter. We went out as a team, so it was a team responsibility. And, it was a team success - a minor success, but a success nonetheless. More importantly we rid half the county of the visual blight - that scourge of the front lawn - the pink eyesore known as the "lawn flamingo." We were deeply concerned of what could transpire if the advance of those dastardly birds went unchecked. It was the classic Domino Theory as it pertains to gaudy lawn ornaments. Once the Pink Menace gets a leg-up in the front yards of the local municipalities then it could possibly infest the rural areas. Just as Ike said, "You have a row of dominoes set up, you knock over the first one, and what will happen to the last one is the certainty that it will go over very quickly. So you could have a beginning of a disintegration that would have the most profound influences." We owed it to the visual sensibilities of our community to act.

It is hard to say who our mentor was. Hogan's Heroes had been on the local NBC affiliate out of Omaha at 1600 hours (that's 4:00 p.m. to civilians) everyday for the first six years of our lives. Naturally, we were well versed in operations in hostile territory, especially against inept adversaries. Although none of us will ever admit to it, The A-Team may have influenced our suspicions of authority and instilled in us the importance of improvisation in the field. Our vehicular daring was reminiscent of The Rat Patrol, but The Dukes of Hazard would paint a more accurate depiction. But, honestly speaking, I don't think we would have believed that a small group of young Americans such as ourselves could have a meaningful impact on our surroundings had we not witnessed the Wolverines rout the Rooskies and Cubans in Red Dawn. Heck, Omaha got nuked - how could that not motivate us?

In retrospect, Operation Yardbird (my personal codename for this first outing for obvious reasons and also in tribute to Hendrix's favorite musicians) was essentially a training mission, a tune-up for later events. During Yardbird we began developing the special bond that is essential for effective strike force teams: our mindsets converged to a single consciousness, our communications evolved to a near telepathic level, our individual strengths intertwined to obscure all weaknesses. We became a lean, mean, spiteful machine.

Late that Saturday night: Hendrix, Cookie, Squid, Rudy, and a freshman apprentice, Gilligan; and, me, too, of course. I had to be there - I was the wheels. We all had vehicles or at least access to vehicles. We had to have vehicles. We live in farm country - we have to drive to everything. But, just as the A-Team had that butt ugly black van, as Sgt's Troy and Moffitt had their olive drab jeep with .50 caliber machine gun, and the Dukes had that indestructible orange Charger replete with racist banner on the roof, we had my truck. To the uninformed, it was just another rusting 1974 Chevrolet Blazer. In actuality it was the ultimate "sleeper" and perfect for our covert ops. The steed we would take into the field was a magnificent beast. That's what we called it: "the Beast." A truck built in a time when you and two friends could sit on the hood and not be concerned about caving it in. A real Chevy built with real steel – you could tell it was real steel because like all General Motor's of the early '70s it had rusted through at all the wheel wells. It would seat eight comfortably and was the size of a humvee before humvees existed. Most important, it had a huge engine. Although the factory had originally powered it sufficiently with a 350 cubic inch normally aspirated power plant, that wasn't quite enough for my father. My father was extolling the virtues of "more power" when Tim "the Tool Man" Allen was still just Timothy "the coke pusher" Allen Dick in the pokey. In addition to the engine swap that my dad did, I installed a disconnect switch to the brake lights and added a red police rotating beacon to the standard Blazer lighting package. As Han Solo once said, "She may not look like much, but she's got it where it counts, kid. I've made a lot of special modifications myself."

Fate gave an ironic nod of the head to President Eisenhower. We set out with the recollection of having seen the Pink Scourge invade lawns at an alarming pace. Apparently our perception had been clouded by our bias: we greatly overestimated the enemy's numbers. Our frontal assault on the pink menace turned into a mission of search and capture. We scoured all eight residential blocks in Mondamin, both residential blocks in River Sioux and Little Sioux, all six residential blocks in Pisgah, and another six blocks of residences in Modale to no avail. Either the entire western half of Harrison County had been tipped off about Operation Yardbird, or we had greatly overestimated the lack of aesthetic sensibility possessed by the majority of the inhabitants of our community. Having driven over one hundred-fifty miles, we had to refuel before heading into the most populous (and heavily patrolled) town in the county, Missouri Valley. In addition to the two Sheriff's deputies with whom we had been playing cat and mouse, there would be as many as three Missouri Valley Municipal Police cruisers on patrol; we would need the extra fuel in case we needed to make a hasty withdrawal.

I have a recurring flashback of that night. I am at the wheel of the Beast. Hendrix is riding shotgun scanning for un-friendlies at our front and front-right. Squid and Cookie are riding in the jump seat, keeping watch of the rear perimeter. We have the tailgate down. Even though we are cruising St. Clair Street in Missouri Valley with engine just idling, the Beast is hardly stealthy. The 454 cubic inches were capable of delivering large amounts of horsepower and the twin glass pack "mufflers" always announced as much. The Beast was uncomfortably loud on this night, but we knew that if the stuff hit the fan and we had to abort, the excess of horsepower would assure a swift retreat. We had captured four targets - two each had been brazenly displayed in front of two other neighborhoods in Mo Valley. We were operating a Search and Capture; Gilligan held on to the spare tire in back, and Rudy rode on the tail gate of the Beast; the spotters and I scanned the area for targets and the authorities. Target locations would be given to Rudy ("Ugly Bird at 5 o'clock"). Rudy, dressed head to toe in black, would leap from the tailgate as we slowly and noisily rolled near the targets and rush them. After ripping them from the earth, he would run back to the Beast, throw them to

Gilligan in the back, and return to his perch on the tailgate. This procedure worked flawlessly for the first four targets.

My flashback, however, is of that last target area and the two captures that were yielded from it. Rudy bailed from the back and ran silently through the dim bluish illumination of a lone street light into the yard containing two of those god-awful looking fake birds. And, then he just disappeared. We were on our second trip around the target block and were really getting nervous. The Beast's twin pipes were doing a fine job of announcing our presence, and Rudy was nowhere to be seen. The mission protocol called for a quick hit-and-run and to abort at the first sign of trouble. Rudy had obviously run into trouble, but we couldn't very well abort until he returned to the truck - we had seen Uncommon Valor and knew you never leave a man behind.

We were nearing the end of the block and needed to make the difficult decision of whether to further risk arousing the suspicions of the indigenous personnel and make a third circuit of the block or to risk another one of our squad to go search for Rudy. It was then that there was a crashing of what sounded like metal pipes in the back of the truck. Then the rear end of the Beast lowered noticeably as though a heavy load had been dropped onto the end gate. This racket was accompanied by Rudy swearing a great deal through tortured breath. As he ordered me to "get us the hell out of here" porch lights came on at the target residence. Our cover was blown. I took the most direct route out of Mo Valley and headed north back to my home, generally at thirty to fifty miles per hour over the posted speed limit, brake lights turned off, headlights only used when absolutely necessary. I had practiced this kind of departure from Mo Valley many times. It was during that rapid ride away from Mo Valley that we learned what Rudy had experienced. Unlike the first abductions in which the targets were pink plastic with spindly wire legs, the last two visual abominations were concrete, approximately twenty-five pounds each, and each had been perched upon two 3-foot long legs of one inch diameter steel rebar. That was about sixty pounds of ugly ornamentation; it was no wonder the Beast had shuddered under the burden.

We arrived back at the evening's base of operations, my home, without detecting any kind of pursuit. To ensure that any authorities who may have just been a little slow in arriving would have nothing out of the ordinary to see, we went into my house and watched the last few skits of Saturday Night Live. I lived several miles outside of Mondamin and had no satellite dish so we were relegated to the realm of network television and the less than inspired fare that the networks broadcast. We sat in silence, not so much because we were drained from the evening's Operation, but because it was the Piscopo years of SNL and the show just wasn't very funny. After the very lame one-hit-wonder band Madness performed some other song we'd never heard before, we shut off the television and went back outside to finish the Operation.

It wasn't enough to just remove garish visage of the Pink Menace from public view. A message had to be sent. Using some concrete blocks of unknown origin as an altar/base for the birds' legs, we set up the spoils of our raid in the driveway of my home. Hendrix and I doused all of the faux-feathered abominations with a gallon of gasoline out of a red plastic two-gallon jug that I had filled for this moment. For actions above and beyond the call of duty, Rudy was unanimously given the honor of tossing the match that would serve as a stern warning to offensive ornamentation everywhere: "Regardless of how many folk-of-little-taste may be out there willing to put you on display for God and everyone to see, there will always be a small but determined group willing to risk driving privileges and possible court costs to eradicate the landscape of your existence." We stood about fifteen feet back as Rudy tossed a match towards the gas soaked obscenities. He missed. Rudy moved a little closer and tossed another match; it glanced off the beak of one of the plastic flamingos and fell harmlessly to the driveway. He moved closer, about five feet away from the would-be pyre, and tossed a third match. The smallish fireball was a thing of beauty. The four plastic birds stood upon their wire legs like flaming lollipops; the black smoke of burning gasoline and smoldering polyvinyl chloride waft through the still night air partially obscuring the security light above the driveway. The concrete birds, on the other hand, were not as easily obliterated. The liquid gasoline merely burned itself out without leaving a mark. We had not expected to generate enough heat to destroy the concrete birds but thought we could blacken them enough to obliterate that putrid pink pigmentation. Recognizing that we were failing at this, Cookie grabbed the gas can and started pouring more fuel onto the birds - even though the other birds were still flaming puddles of plastic just below the rebar legs of the concrete flamingos. Most of the gas he poured did indeed splash onto the remaining two birds; however, a good portion of the gas also splashed onto the flaming remnants of the other four birds.

Although what happened next probably only took a fraction of a second, what I witnessed appeared to occur in slow motion. The residual flames in the now smoldering oily puddles that had once been plastic birds ignited the gas dripping from the underside of the concrete birds. The dripping gas became a liquid fuse of sorts to the main payload, the fuel that had soaked into the pores of the concrete birds. The gas soaked birds erupted into a gaseous fireball which nearly singed all the hair off Cookie.

The ensuing carnage didn't end there; Cookie was still pouring when the birds ignited. The stream of gas coming out of the gas can's nozzle caught fire. The flames followed the stream of fuel from the birds back to the nozzle. It was like seeing the flamethrowers in the final battle of The Sands of Iwo Jima but only in reverse.

Cookie dropped the gas can onto the asphalt driveway and jumped back. The can landed upright, and a small flame burned at the end of the nozzle. The driveway was already awash in the orange light from the still flaming concrete birds - finally turning a nice shade of charcoal - and the red plastic can sat there like an oil lamp, adding to the gasoline light. We all knew there was still some liquid gas in the can as well as the fumes that were fueling the lamp-like fire at the end of the nozzle. An explosion was inevitable. But, before any of us had even begun to retreat to a safer distance, Rudy again went into action.

Whether it was a complete disregard for personal safety or just a total lack of forethought, Rudy ran to the flaming gas can and did a Karate Kid kick at the nozzle. His kick "blew" out the flame and eliminated the immediate danger. We all breathed a collective sigh of relief. It was agreed that we had achieved an adequate level of blackness on the concrete flamingos. The four black, bubbling Frisbee-sized puddles of ooze that had once been plastic flamingos had cooled sufficiently to peel nicely off the driveway and throw into the garbage. We enjoyed a beverage or two while the concrete flamingos burned away the rest of the gasoline and cooled. Now quite drained from what we all agreed was just a bit more excitement than any young person should be allowed to have in one evening, everyone climbed into their cars and headed home for much needed rest. I threw the blackened carcasses of the concrete flamingos into a road ditch out in the country, where I presume they remain today.

The Wednesday edition of the Missouri Valley times had a one-paragraph article about the success of our Operation. Granted, it was in the Police Blotter section of the paper detailing a loss complaint that was filed, but it was publicity just the same.

We made a statement. Would it be heeded? As of last week, an avenging garden troll and his tacky lawn ornament minions overtook a yard near where I grew up. The answer is "no," we were not heard.

200

More importantly, however, is that we saw what we perceived to be a wrong being perpetrated upon our community and we banded together, developed a plan, and executed it. We acted and the Red Flag Commandos were born.

Like most subversive organizations, after making our initial splash statement, we went into deep cover to allow our message to settle in - and, to allow the enthusiasm to apprehend and punish to wane. Additionally, we had no idea what we should do for an encore.

Intoxicated (mostly) by the success of the triumph of Operation Yardbird, the Commandos were eager for another foray into the field. However, it would be weeks before a cause worthy of our intervention would present itself. Plus, with the media coverage we had received the authorities were most certainly going to making a half-hearted effort to find the abductors of the pink scourge; so we decided to continue our civilian personas, hiding in plain site, as it were.

I arrived at Rudy's late one Friday night five months after Operation Yardbird. The fall night was crisp and calm. Sarge lay on the driveway, blood oozing from his cheek and forearm. He massaged a fresh shiner appearing around his left eye with a cold, unopened can of beer.

"Hey, Sarge."

"Hey."

I stepped over him and headed to the house. I had to sidle past Hendrix and Cookie who were trying to reattach a damaged screen door to the front of the house. There was a patch of skin stuck to a tear at the center of the screen. I had to ask: "Did he win the bet?"

"What do you think?"

I had missed it. Since it was too cool for the ceiling fan to be on, Gilligan, a friend of Rudy's, bet Sarge a beer that he couldn't dive through the screen door. As before, Sarge "won" the bet and received a beer for the effort. A can of beer that Sarge bought in the first place.

I glanced at the television and saw that it was tuned to some pedestrian network television show. I could have seen that at my home. What the hell?

"What the hell?" I said, gesturing to the television.

"Scrambled," was Rudy's reply. "They started scrambling the good satellite stations."

The bastards.

"The bastards," I said.

We knew that the days of free satellite television programming would eventually come to an end; we just never thought it would be so soon. It was the cruel reality of entertainment economics giving us the finger. Large metropolitan areas with several broadcast television stations with strong, clear signals were the first places to get cable television. Thank goodness those big cities were serviced first. Places the likes of Blair and Missouri Valley had only had cable for a year or two. The remote and rural areas such as ours would be last; our places were considered too small of a market to support cable television. I guess the handful of isolated satellite dish owners were too large of an economic drain to ignore. I had to step outside for air.

Sarge was still on the ground, now drinking the beer he "won" for destroying the screen door. Hendrix and Cookie finished reattaching the screen door to the house. The tear in the screen flapped lazily in the autumn breeze. Good thing the mosquitoes were done in by the early hard freeze. Squid pulled into the driveway when I was hit with another mild Tourette's moment.

"Those stingy, big city, rat bastards," I said, throwing my hat at the satellite dish.

It was a childish and futile gesture, accomplishing nothing, and it did not make me feel better. The man was sticking it to the rural folks again, hitting us where it hurt the most, television; there was nothing the typical small town resident could do.

Squid wanted to know why I was throwing my hat at inanimate objects. Again. Cookie told him about the scrambling. He understood immediately. Rudy's dish was an entertainment lifeline for us. We could not stay sane by having Sarge doing stupid things to win back his own beer forever. We would try, of course, but eventually that would lose its appeal.

"We have to do something," Squid said.

202

"Maybe it's time to implement Operation Moonman."

"You ain't gonna make me stick my head in the ceiling fan, again are you?" Sarge asked.

"No, not this time, Sarge. Not this time."

I reached over and hung my hat on the receiving horn of Rudy's satellite dish. The television screen inside turned to snowy static. And, just like that, the wheels were put into motion to do the Mission.

The genesis of Operation Moonman was the accidental discovery of Missouri Valley's satellite downlink facility that fed Ultravision, their cable television monopoly. They were the only cable television provider for Missouri Valley and the entire county. Their service, however, did not extend beyond the city limits. Their subscribers were quite smug about having entertainment options the rest of the county could only imagine. As if the rest of the county needed another excuse to dislike them.

Their arrogance would be their undoing. As much as the citizens loved their dozens of clear television channels Ultravision provided, they would not tolerate the aesthetically repulsiveness of the equipment needed to turn them into couch potatoes. Hendrix and I found the somewhat secluded facility just beyond their city limits on a seldom-used secondary road leading into the Loess Hills. Our low paying, part-time cover jobs with the County Road Department did have some benefits.

This was to be our target. It wasn't very large; a small compound about fifty feet wide and maybe seventy-five feet long area of gravel with a tiny, white, windowless shack in its center. There were three or four large satellite dishes – much larger in diameter than Rudy's – and three or four small, eight foot diameter dishes, and a whole bunch of radio antennas all around the shack. A superficial effort had been made to "secure" the area: the compound was surrounded by a short chain link fence topped by a couple of strands of barbed-wire. And, a small warning sign was attached to the gate. Like that would keep the commandos from making a statement. "Keep Out – No Trespassing" indeed.

We brainstormed mission plans ever since we discovered the site. It was before the internet, what with its satellite photos, detailed maps, and conspiracy web sites. The justification for our deeds would have to be homegrown. Our intell would be gathered from personal reconnaissance. Our plans would have to be based upon careful study of tactics used in "Force 10 from Navarone," new episodes of "The A-Team," and reruns of "Hogan's Heroes."

Deep down we knew that neither Ultravision nor the citizens of Missouri Valley had anything to do with the heartless entertainment conglomerates cutting free reception of the satellite signals. But, we knew that a statement, albeit a somewhat childish and ambiguous one, should be made. And sticking it to the largest town in the county wouldn't bother the other much smaller towns and rural residents one iota.

Cookie, Hendrix, and I performed the first recon, scouting out the vicinity to get a feel for the area, the terrain, possible hidden security systems, and unanticipated potential pitfalls. We used the classic broken down car ruse to appear inconspicuous during our reconnoiter. Ordinarily we would have used my truck for this but since my truck would be our transport for the mission itself we felt it best to keep it away from the target until T-time. My truck looked perfectly natural on the roadside with its hood open and me looking pissed off at the world. Cookie's old Chevette looked only slightly less plausible. So, there we were, about 100 yards from the fenced compound, parked in a cornfield driveway, with Cookie's 'vette looking broken.

While Cookie stood in front of his car looking at the engine, Hendrix and I hopped down into the road ditch to make a stealthy scan of the neighborhood. Our silent approach to the compound was anything but that. I began our recon by getting tangled in the remnants of an old barbed wire fence hiding in low brush near the top of the ditch. After tearing my jeans on the fence and stumbling into a second fence near the other side of the ditch, the profane tirade I was muttering under my breath was completely drowned out by an incessant crunching. Being late fall, the ditch was filled with dry dormant grass and dead leaves. Sounding like a bad Grape Nuts commercial, we crunched our way to the equipment shack surrounded by satellite dishes. The racket we made would definitely have to be minimized during the actual mission.

In less than 30 seconds we were at the fence. We stopped and looked at the chain link fence that out-sized us by a foot with three runs of barbed wire jutting out another 12 inches above the chain link. Additional warning signs were wired to the fence gently reminding potential trespassers to "Keep Out." Inside the secure area were two satellite dishes that were about twice as tall as the fence and several others the same size as the one at Rudy's house. As we studied this galvanized steel fabric barrier separating us from the dishes we noticed that even though we had stopped to study the fence's integrity, there was still crunching of leaves and grass in the ditch. Moving fast. And, getting closer. Really fast.

Just seconds after realizing we were being chased, a horse of a dog bounded up and bared his fangs at us. The ensuing growling sparked us into action. We ran. We also abandoned all pretenses of stealth and concealment. We sprinted down the middle of the gravel road towards the car, shouting at Cookie to open the doors and start the engine as the vicious mutt snapped at our hind sections. I chanced a glance over my shoulder at the vile beast and saw that a house further north up the road had a perfect view of our predicament, but I didn't see anyone in the picture window witnessing the impromptu track meet.

We dove into the car through the doors Cookie had left open for us, hitting the dog in the muzzle as we slammed them shut. The dog circled the car menacingly, occasionally leaping at the windows. After a few minutes of pacing, Cujo began to trot way, stopping every few feet to turn and glare at us. Stupid furbag. It eventually disappeared into a hedge lining the lawn of a house in the area a few hundred yards south of the target. We waited a few minutes to allow our pulses to stabilize. Cookie restarted the car, and we departed the area.

On the surface it may appear that the recon was a failure. But, quite to the contrary, we gathered a considerable amount of intel on our target. We learned the locations of the camouflaged barbed wire fences, the potential pitfall presented by the natural alarm system of dried foliage in the ditch bottom, the size of the satellite dishes, the height of the fence, and most importantly, the size and disposition of the neighbor's dog.

Hendrix created the mission map using this wealth of reconnaissance data. Penciled in was the highway, the gravel road, the compound, the house to the north, the house to the south (with a note about the dog), the ditch, both barbed wire fences, and jagged lines where the timber was located. It was really more a sketch of the area but it was drawn on blue-lined grid paper like the military maps used as props in the movies. Not to any discernible scale, no legend, and the topography information was guesstimated, but since it was on grid paper, that made it a map.

The map was presented to the group at the next gathering at Rudy's place. Rudy, Squid, Cookie, Gilligan, Hendrix, and I were present; Sarge hadn't arrived yet. From all the obstacles glaring at us in Number 2 pencil lead on the grid paper, we knew this operation would require exquisite timing and precise execution for our infiltration, neutralization, and extraction to be accomplished without attracting attention. There was no room for screw-ups.

The names have been omitted from the following dialog to provide minimal anonymity.

"Will we use a rolling insertion or go with another broken down car ruse?"

"Rolling to minimize the chance of attracting the attention of the neighbors or some do-gooder mechanic wannabe."

"What about driver, then?"

"That's covered already."

"Shouldn't we have someone on point in case there is more barbed wire missed during recon?"

"There's a timber we should cut through. It'll provide cover, and there won't be any fences in it."

"How about the compound gate. We need someone to move in ahead of the main team with a bolt cutter to clip the lock."

"Nope. That would give away our entry. The humans on V the other night got into the same type of facility just by throwing a wool blanket on the fence's barbed wire and climbed right over."

"You watch that show?"

"Screw you, butt wipe."

"First two men to the compound should have the blankets then."

"And the dog? Won't we need a decoy to preoccupy the mutt?"

"I think pellet guns would be safer. Reach out from long range if it gets too close. A low power thump should make it stay away."

"Two guys with pellet rifles should be plenty."

"Lookout?"

"The riflemen will have primary lookout duties. Blanket men will have eyes peeled, too."

"What about the dish work in the compound?"

"The two small guys will do that. They're the quickest and should have an easier time with the fence. The blanket men can toss the supplies to them once the perimeter is breached."

"Mission time?"

"Five minutes?"

"Ten minutes?"

"From drop-off to extraction it shouldn't take more than ten minutes."
"Better call it fifteen then."

"Agreed."

"OK, but we're back to the original question."

"We've got two dishmen, two blanket men, two riflemen, and a driver. That's seven."

"We could go with one blanket man."

"Not good. We should have full operational redundancy."

"Then we need a second driver and second truck."

"Shut up, asshole. Too much traffic on that stretch of road would bring unwanted attention."

"OK, then almost full operational redundancy except for the most important job."

"Right."

"That makes seven."

"There are seven of us."

"More like six and a half."

"So what do we do?"

"Nut's brother has a Suburban."

"Nut?"

"Sure. He'd be good for this. Dependable. Will keep his mouth shut. And, a bigger truck for the insertion."

"Any objections?"

"Then it's decided. Nut's our new wheel man and we are not bringing Sarge in on this one."
All heads were nodding.

"Maybe we just send Sarge on a beer run and have him meet us at the staging area after the mission."

"Gentlemen, the operational security of the team and the overall likelihood of mission success has just been greatly enhanced."

"When do we go?"

"Sooner would be better."

"Next Friday?"

"Saturday would be better."

"Why?"

"I have a date."

"OK, asshole, Saturday then. We need two blankets, two pellet guns, and dark clothes. We assemble at 2000 hours, gear check at 2015, roll at 2030, insertion at 2055, pickup at 2110, and be back at the staging area cracking open a cold one by 2130."

And, with that the mission planning was done. By the time Sarge arrived we were watching Friday Night Videos on NBC – nothing on the remaining unscrambled satellite stations was of interest. We made no mention of the planning session.

We worked out additional details during the week. Nut enthusiastically agreed to join the team and to get his brother's Suburban for the mission. This relieved me of driver duties and allowed me to become one of the riflemen/lookouts. As much as I enjoyed being a wheelman I really wanted to be on the ground for this one.

Cookie would be the other rifleman and lookout. Hendrix and Squid would take care of the blankets for the fence and get the supplies into the compound. Rudy and Gilligan, our two toughest, smallest, and quickest team members were going over the fence.

The map was handed from team member to team member throughout the week for study. The most concealed point near the facility was marked in ink with an "X" where Nut would slow the truck down so we could jump out of the truck and not be seen by the home to the north. We would hop the first barbed wire fence cross the ditch, hop the second fence and regroup in the timber. Hendrix and Squid would lead the squad to the compound, followed by Rudy and Gilligan, with Cookie and me covering the rear watching for the dog. Nut would take the truck up the gravel road about two miles to an intersection where he would turn around and hold position. Just as discussed during the planning session, Squid and Hendrix would throw the wool blankets onto the barbed wire jutting out at the top of the fence and help Rudy and Gilligan up the fence. Once Rudy and Gilligan were inside, Hendrix and Squid would toss the supplies over the fence where Gilligan and Rudy would then knock out communications. Once the equipment was incapacitated, Gilligan and Rudy would toss any remaining equipment back over the fence, climb up and over the fence, grabbing the blankets on the way down. Squid and Hendrix would secure the supplies and then the group would make its way back to the pick-up point, where Nut would presumably be approaching at the fifteen-minute mark. Cookie and I would cover pellet fire as needed if the dog approached and would sound alarm at the sight of human eyes. The squad would be wearing black and would duck into the shadows of the trees in the timber if necessary; Rudy and Gilligan would have the most exposure inside the compound but there were plenty of dishes to duck behind to provide them concealment. The pick up point would be on the opposite side of the road from the facility, about 100 yards south of the compound. Nut would slow the Suburban down again and we would climb back aboard on the roll. Nut would then drive us – at the speed limit – back to the staging area (my home) where Sarge should be waiting with beer. A simple plan in which the biggest variable was the choice of beverage we would have at the post-mission celebration.

A good plan can be executed by the most mediocre of squads. To make a bad plan work requires a good team. That night we were a very good team.

Who would have imagined that three minutes of hurried reconnaissance and a mission map sketched on an old sheet of graph paper would produce a plan that would disintegrate at such an alarming rate?

Our operational parameters were altered three days before the Mission. A weather front moved through our theater of operations and blanketed the area with snow. Continued cold weather ensured the snow remained at mission time.

The remainder of the week was uneventful. The person with the date got stood up, but the rest of the team insisted on keeping Saturday as our Mission night out of jealous spite.

Nut, Squid, Rudy, and I decided we would rally at Rudy's place. Squid and I were early but Rudy was ready to hit it. Nut was late. The mission schedule was hosed, and we hadn't even loaded up. We still had to pick up Cookie, Hendrix, and Gilligan in Modale.

Ten minutes after roll time, Nut arrived. In his red Ford Escort.

Squid exploded. "Nut, what the hell? Where's the Suburban?"

"Brother has it still. Sorry."

"For shit's sake," I said. "We'll take my truck and make do. Nut, you're still the wheel man." I wasn't about to give up my position on the ground for this mission.

We loaded the mission supplies into my truck, and Nut drove us to Modale. It was a very quiet seven miles. We were late and in a truck much smaller than we had envisioned. Nut was more than a little embarrassed.

Things got worse at Cookie's house. Hendrix and Gilligan were waiting outside when we pulled in to Cookie's driveway. They were staring at their feet looking a little sheepish. Cookie was still inside. He came out the front door carrying his air rifle as Gilligan and Hendrix squeezed into the truck. Cookie's mother followed him outside telling him to keep warm and to not get caught.

Don't get caught?

"Cookie, man, say you didn't tell your mom about the mission," I implored.

"Of course I told my parents – we don't have secrets. Besides, what if we get caught? Someone will have to bail us out of jail."

He may have had a small point about the bailing out thing; we had no contingency plans for being apprehended. We assumed we would be successful. This breach of operational security was starting to show that failure was indeed an option.

We did a quick check before leaving Cookie's place. All personnel and gear were present and operational. It was already 23 minutes past our planned roll time. Since our scheduled mission time was chosen arbitrarily, this wasn't overly important, just disconcerting. Nut put my truck into "Drive" and we were off to the Ultravision compound.

The drive down Interstate 29 was devoid of conversation. I would like to say it was because we were psyching ourselves up by visualizing the mission but that would be inaccurate. It was partly because we were a little peeved with Cookie for being so damned flippantly open with his parents about covert actions and partly because the notion of being caught was creeping into everyone's thoughts because instead of olive drab wool blankets for breaching the fence we had disturbingly multicolored patchwork quilts. However, the silence was mostly because of the particularly good tunes emanating from the single in-dash speaker of my truck (Z-92.3 FM was living up to its slogan of being "The Rock"). We passed through Missouri Valley to the sound of Dire Strait's Money for Nothing.

Go time. We approached the target and immediately saw that we had a problem. We had planned our entry to be via a slow moving Suburban which would have allowed the team jump out of three doors and the rear tailgate on the roll; it would only take seconds. My truck didn't have that many doors. We had to stop the truck. Two minutes later the team and supplies were on the ground. Nut drove slowly away while we bolted for the timber. In the distance a dog barked.

The temperature was near zero, making every rapid, nervous breath we took painfully visible. The four inches of snow on the ground - so far - muffled the sound of the dried leaves and grass we had to cross to get to the timber. We made it past the barbed wire fences to the tree line and through the timber to the compound fence without losing anyone. Except for the exposure exiting the truck things had gone well. We were four minutes into the Mission, at the perimeter of the target, and poised to breach fence. Cookie and I took up our positions at the corners of the fence and pumped up our rifles twice. We liked animals so we kept the rifles at low power, hoping that a stinging warning would be enough to discourage the dog from attacking us. I considered thumping Cookie with a shot – I was still pissed with his lack of discipline. A dog barked again and sounded closer.

Hendrix and Squid tossed the quilts onto the barbed wire above us. Rudy and Gilligan climbed up the chain link and gingerly tossed a leg over the blanket. Their insulated pants and the blankets provided just enough protection to keep them from getting ensnared at the top of the fence. After getting their privates and legs over the barbed wire, they dropped to the ground. They were in. I heard a barking dog nearby.

Squid and Hendrix lobbed the supplies over the fence to Gilligan and Rudy. They grabbed the packs and walked towards the two large satellite dishes. We all looked at one another. It was the point of no return. Rudy shot us a gloved thumbs-up. We all gave the same in reply. And that stupid dog sounded very close.

Then the plan really started to crumble.

Hendrix, Squid, Cookie, and I stood watch with our backs to the fence, eyes scanning the gravel road for overly curious traffic. The dog had stopped barking and that worried me. Then from inside the fence Rudy unleashed a string of expletives rivaled only by an Eddie Murphy stand-up act that pierced the silence of the frigid night. We turned in unison to view what could possibly be worthy of profanely announcing our presence.

"Would you shut the hell up?"

"It ain't working," he hissed back. "The damn tape won't stick."

We knew from our recon that the main dishes were quite a bit different from the one at Rudy's place. Rudy's dish had a receiver "horn" held out in front of the dish by an aluminum arm. The horn was the size of a soup can, easily covered by a ball cap. The main target dishes, however, were totally different animals. They had three arms attached to the outer edge of the dish that came together at a point about eight feet in front of the dish. But, instead of a horn, there was a cone shaped reflector attached to the nexus of these arms that pointed back to the inside of the dish. The horn was a long, slender rectangular protrusion, about 8 inches on a side, sticking out of the center of the dish about five feet. We knew even if we swiped a couple of hats from our gentle giant of a friend, Flash, they still wouldn't be large enough to cover the larger dishes' horns. Besides, we didn't want to leave anything that would point the authorities to hooligans outside Missouri Valley's usual suspects or to any acquaintances of ours. So our plan was the epitome of simplicity: we would duct tape aluminum pie pans to the horns. We figured the aluminum would effectively block out the signal to provide our desired disruption of service and that the duct tape would hold firmly yet with an annoying amount of effort could be removed. Our goal was to make a point, not permanently damage. The dishes were pointed at about a 30-degree angle from the ground with the lower edge of the dish being just a couple feet above the snow. Rudy and Gilligan each had climbed into the bowl of a dish and were standing next to the horns, both looking miffed.

What we neglected to take into consideration, however, was how dusty and cold the horns would be that night. This was why Rudy was cursing. Gilligan was equally stymied but much less demonstrative about it. Our plan appeared to be hosed.

Then Squid took action. Without saying a word, he scaled the fence, gingerly crossed over one of the quilts, and jumped into the compound. This was not part of the mission plan. He reached into the supply bag, pulled out a small box, and strode over to Gilligan's dish and climbed onto it. Hendrix and I looked at each other puzzled. I looked at Cookie; he was petting that damned dog.

Squid wrapped his right leg around the horn (thankfully it didn't bend or, worse yet, break off completely) and opened up the small box he pulled from the bag. And, then he started unreeling a long, malleable sheet, covering the end of the horn in a blanket of silver. Squid had Reynolds Wrapped the horn.

No one knew he had included the box of aluminum foil with the pie pans and duct tape – it wasn't part of the Mission Plan. He did it on a whim – the pans and foil were sitting near each other in the store. After covering Gilligan's dish he lobbed the box over to Rudy who quickly did the same to his. He then ran around the compound covering the horns on the smaller dishes. Gilligan packed up the unused pie pans and useless duct tape and tossed the supply bag back over the fence. He and Squid climbed over the fence and out of the compound while Rudy put the finishing touches on the remaining dishes. The dog was lying at Cookie's feet.

It seemed like we had been there for hours but it had actually been less than eight minutes. Things appeared to be back on track; even with the duct tape snafu, Squid's improvisation put us ahead of schedule. Then Rudy got hung up at the top of the fence while trying to remove the quilts from the barbed wire. After a copious amount of tugging and cursing he tumbled to the ground clutching both blankets. Only a scrap of Kansas Star was left entangled in the barbs. The dog appeared to be dozing now.

We scrambled back to the timber and moved close to the tree line to wait for extraction. But, it had been just over ten minutes and Nut would be another five minutes out. We were relatively out of sight, but with the objective completed we were anxious to vacate the area. Three minutes ahead of schedule we saw headlights coming back down the road. Nut was early; despite his lack of respect for the plan, we were grateful to be getting the hell away from the target. Even though several of the mission plan details had gone awry, it appeared we were finally out of the woods.

As the headlights drew closer, we broke out from our cover and sprinted to the opposite side of the road to await extraction. The other side of the road was a steep, snow-covered embankment with only a few small trees. We were totally exposed when we realized that it wasn't Nut in my truck that was approaching. Shit.

"Shit! It's not Nut! Take cover!"

We threw ourselves prone to the slope hoping to blend into the topography. The effort was futile. As done in every Hogan's Heroes episode we had seen, we were all clad in black and dark blues; excellent camouflage in the shadows of trees and satellite dishes but totally worthless on a snow covered slope bathed in moonlight. Gilligan crouched behind a small thicket but was still only partially shielded. The rest of us helplessly pressed our dark forms into the white of the slope. We were literally trying to hide in plain sight.

There was no way we wouldn't be seen by the car passing by us twenty feet away. Shit. Shit. Shit.

Somehow that car passing just twenty feet away did not see us. Perhaps they just didn't care that there was a squad of independent thinking, militant activists cowering in the snow. Or maybe they were preoccupied with avoiding the barking dog that was running along side the driver's side of the car. Either way, the people in the car didn't so much as glance our way as they passed.

We remained frozen in place, deceiving ourselves that pressing our dark clothed frames into the snow had made us invisible. The night's frigid air gave away that we were all hyperventilating with relief. A rumbling motor approaching stirred us from our "hiding" place.

Nut pulled up to where we had taken conspicuous refuge, fifteen minutes – fifteen minutes exactly - from the time he had dropped us at the target. The radio in my truck had been changed to the local pop 'n' roll station; Styx's Snow Blind blared from my dash.

Hendrix, Cookie, and I jumped into the truck through the passenger door as Rudy and Gilligan entered through the end gate. The air in the truck held an acrid stench. It was from a cheap cigar Nut was smoking. He glanced around the truck to make sure we were all onboard and said "I love it when a plan comes together," before gunning the engine and taking us away from the target.

Nut drove us through the heart of the enemy, right down the main thoroughfare of Missouri Valley, before taking a state highway to my place. During the fifteen-minute drive down the winding asphalt pavement skirting the Loess Hills, the realization of our monumental accomplishment slowly started to manifest itself. As far as we knew, we had just disabled the television reception of almost every household in the largest town in our county.

As Nut moved us away from the target, the mission tension gradually eased, smug satisfaction creeping in first, then replaced with unabashed jubilation. Bon Jovi's Dead or Alive drifted out the in-dash speaker, a staticy prediction of our future.

We struck another blow for decency. And we made a clean getaway. Our schedule was totally blown. Our planned transport was not available. Our internal security was breached. Our canine nemesis had doubled on us and turned ally. Our method of disruption was improvised. Our presence was nearly discovered. Our mission plan was a disaster. But, with skill, cunning, and a large dose of good fortune, we had persevered. Now it was time to celebrate.

In keeping with the theme of the night, Sarge – and the beer he was supposed to provide – was nowhere to be found. The final part of the Mission was, fittingly, botched. Fortunately, the emergency beverage supply I had at my house was just enough to celebrate our triumph – a final ad-lib to our dismal plan. So, celebrate we did.

The following day Hendrix provided what we considered the coup de gras: a letter made of letters cut out of old magazines declaring that cable television was capitalism at its most evil and that vengeance had been exacted by the Red Flag Commandos – and further action would be exacted if this brazen discrimination against the small communities continues. It was beautiful. The team smiled and nodded when asked if it should be sent. It went in the mail that day, addressed to the local newspaper.

The next edition of said paper confirmed our success with the following article:

Vandals Foiled Ultravision
Cable television service throughout the city Saturday night was interrupted for several hours when vandals covered Ultravision's satellite dishes with tinfoil. Ultravision was alerted to the service disruption but took several hours to discover the unusual source of the disruption. Ultravision has offered a $50 reward for information leading to the arrest and conviction of the perpetrator or perpetrators.

The confirmation of the success of the Mission was bittersweet. The acknowledgment of our action was quite satisfying; however, the magazine letter manifesto was not mentioned, and they referred to us as common vandals - an insult to our organization. Most disturbing, though, was the reward. Perhaps we were a bit shortsighted, but the bounty on our collective heads was most unexpected.

The day that article appeared was the day the Red Flag Commandos disbanded and went into deep cover. It was the mid 80's and fifty bucks was fifty bucks. We knew no one in the group would turn stoolie, but we could trust no one else. Operation Moonman was the last mission we ever undertook.

I would like to believe that our effort did bear fruit. It was not long after the Mission that towns the size of Mondamin and Modale got cable television service, finally fulfilling Dire Strait's demand by providing the small towns their MTV (although the money for nothing and chicks for free still elude most small town residents). I also heard rumors that the Missouri Valley hospital reported a statistical spike in the birth rate approximately nine months after the mission. I can't say for certain that the Red Flag Commandos are directly responsible for all the children born during that "surge" but I have to admit when the television is out in a rural setting the entertainment options are somewhat limited.

The group returned to hiding in plain sight. We gradually entered mainstream occupations that kept our participation in Operation Moonman concealed yet allowed us to subtly monitor for any possible detection of our identities. Some of us stayed in the area, leading productive, respected lives. The rest of us scattered across the nation, watching from a distance for any sign of pursuit of the Commandos. It is our hope that the variety of covers we now have will offer us at least a small warning should interested parties ever discover our identities.

To this day, over twenty years later, none of us can cover leftovers in Reynolds Wrap without smiling. We all live with the fear that somehow, some way, someone will discover our true identities and piece together the puzzle we call Operation Moonman and turn us in for the fifty smackers.

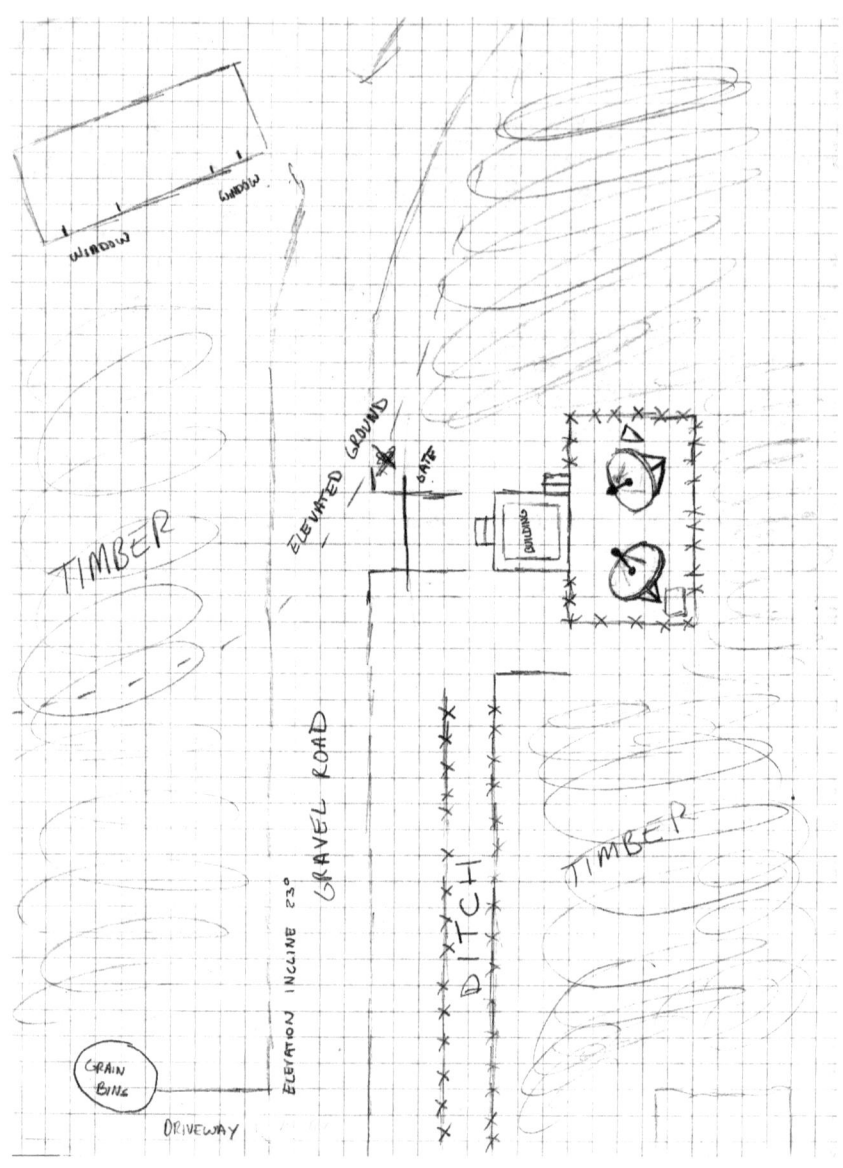

The Mission Map

Songs

Jeffrey D. Deitering

It was late one Friday
I was out with the boys when
the radio played that one funny song
by that one Weird guy.
We laughed so hard
it brought tears to our eyes.
When I hear that song now
I can't explain why
sometimes that funny song makes me cry.

Late one gray, chilly day
I stood with friends by our cars.
Her family had played a song
thanking the Keeper of the Stars.
I stood silent
looking for the reason why.
When I hear that song now
I don't even try
that sad song will always make me cry.

We stood up front that Saturday
surrounded by those we love.
The organ and those words
rang out from above.
It was the most special day
of our young lives.
When I hear that song now
I look to Him in the sky
that joyous song sometimes makes me cry.

It can happen any time
or on any day.
A sound, a word, a tune
something I hear the radio play.
Memories of places or friends
buried in the songs of our lives.
When I hear those songs now
I understand why
Happy songs sometimes will make me cry.

To Order Copies of

Hooligan from the Hills:
Growing Up Ornery in Iowa's Loess Hills

Visit the author's web sites:

http://www.jdsqrd.com
http://jdsqrd.blogspot.com

or

Contact the author by email:

jdsqrd@ymail.com

www.ingramcontent.com/pod-product-compliance
Lightning Source LLC
Chambersburg PA
CBHW061355280526
45784CB00001B/260